ROOMS

ROOMS
CREATING LUXURIOUS, LIVABLE SPACES

MARIETTE HIMES GOMEZ

ReganBooks

An Imprint of HarperCollinsPublishers

PHOTOGRAPHY CREDITS

Peter Aaron: 87, 88, 178, 201; Antoine Bootz: 216 (top), 224 (bottom), 237 (right); Andrew Bordwin: 243;
Billy Cunningham: vi, 62, 220; Phillip Ennis: 244, 247; Pieter Estersohn: v, viii, 6, 10 (bottom), 11, 12, 15–21,
23, 32, 35, 36, 38, 43, 44, 60, 63, 67, 75, 78–81, 82, 89, 92–101, 110–15, 119, 123, 127, 131–35, 138 (bottom),
142–47, 152–58, 160, 161 (bottom), 162–65, 174–77, 190–93, 196 (right), 198, 202 (left), 212–14, 216
(bottom), 218, 219, 221–24 (top), 230, 238, 239, 241, 248; Scott Frances: 2, 24, 27–29, 31, 34, 45, 59, 65, 76,
83, 90, 102–109, 116, 128, 130, 161 (top), 167, 180, 182–86, 188, 194, 195, 197, 202 (right), 207 (bottom),
210, 217, 237 (left), 240, 242; Gomez Associates: 46; Lizzie Himmel: 8, 9, 54, 84, 124, 125, 126 (right), 203,
206, 215, 225, 228, 236 (left); Thibault Jeanson: 10 (top); Maura McEvoy: 159 (photograph first appeared in
Metropolitan Home); James Mortimer: 85, 126 (left), 168–71, 173, 231 (top); Elizabeth Zeschin: 68, 70, 71–73,
151, 196 (left), 205, 236 (right).

The following photographs have been reprinted by permission from *House Beautiful*, Hearst Communications,
Inc. All Rights Reserved. *House Beautiful*, copyright ©: March 1993, Antoine Bootz, photographer: 64, 207
(top); October 1993, Lizzie Himmel, photographer: 235; November 1993, Thibault Jeanson, photographer:
139, 141, 227; November 1995, Thibault Jeanson, photographer: 120, 208; June 1997, Peter Margonelli, photographer: 136, 138 (top), 231 (bottom); August 1998, Thibault Jeanson, photographer: 4, 232; November
1998, Thibault Jeanson, photographer: ii, 41, 47, 48–51, 53, 56, 57; January 2000, Laura Resen, photographer:
149, 150.

HarperCollins books may be purchased for educational, business, or sales promotional use. For information
please write: Special Markets Department, HarperCollins Publishers Inc., 10 East 53rd Street,
New York, NY 10022.

FIRST EDITION

DESIGNED BY JOEL AVIROM AND JASON SNYDER
DESIGN ASSISTANT: MEGHAN DAY HEALEY

Printed on acid-free paper

Library of Congress Cataloging-in-Publication Data

Gomez, Mariette Himes.
    Rooms: creating luxurious, livable spaces / Mariette Himes Gomez.—1st ed.
      p. cm.
    ISBN 0-06-008370-0
    1. Interior decoration. I. Title.

NK2110 .G627 2003
747—dc21

                                                                                    2002037038

03 04 05 06 07 ❖/IM 10 9 8 7 6 5 4 3 2 1

When you're building a room,
you're building character,
and character is the strength
and wisdom of a home.

CONTENTS

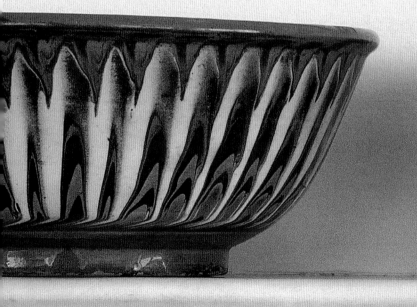

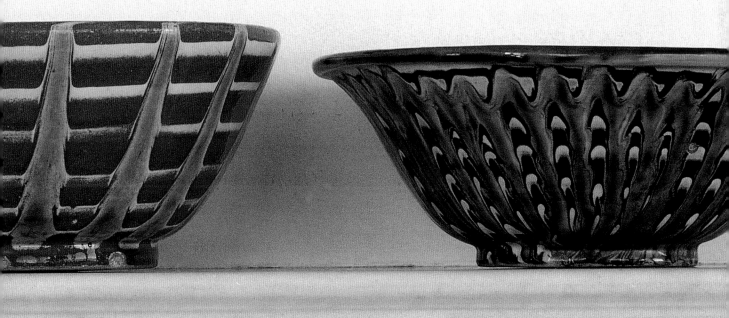

INTRODUCTION: Luxury You Can Live With

AFTER DECADES SPENT helping people decorate their houses, I recently had to confront my own home. In rapid succession, I bought an old question-mark-of-a-house in the country and traded in one Manhattan apartment for another—it was like the cobbler finally getting around to his own shoes, or the doctor prescribing her own medicine.

A house is in some ways an autobiography, a work in progress for a life in progress. Preoccupied with work for others, I had let my own living quarters slip onto automatic pilot. Of course, I would bring in new things from time to time—chairs are my fetish, and paintings my love—but I faced two entirely new living situations, and I had to take charge. The shift from helping others to helping myself was like suddenly looking at the fine print on the back of food packages. As in advertising, there's truth in decorating: I had to figure out what is important to me in my own home—what hurts and what helps in creating a space that can sustain my spirits and enhance my daily routine. I understood firsthand how bewildering all the ingredients in the complex recipe can be.

I took notes, which became an informal diary. Starting from zero, in an empty space, I realized that decorating is a process, not

I rebuilt the gate and restored the original neoclassical detailing on the front porch of the 1790s home I bought in Remsenburg, Long Island. Now the house presents a fine face to the road.

In my former apartment, I didn't really have a foyer, just a small vestibule. I had no room for a console table, so a bracketed shelf took its place. Underneath it, I set a favorite chair. The final result was a lesson in composition, all about squares and circles, dark and light, color as an accent.

just a look or a style. I would like to invite anyone else facing those blank walls into my process. Making a house into a home, especially a beautiful one, is not easy, but neither is it an unsolvable mystery. It starts with building rooms.

Everyone works so hard and moves so fast these days that when we come home, we want to sink into the nearest sofa and feel utterly at peace. Some designers just keep on adding flounces and

furnishings until a room turns into a stage set. I design the kind of rooms where you sit back against the softest, most comfortable cushions and sigh. You're content because, just where you want it, there's a light bright enough to read by and a table on which to set your drink. This is luxury you can live with. I take a very practical approach to personal style. A tastefully decorated, gracefully comfortable home is accessible to anyone with the will to edit, the energy to move furniture around, and the openness to absorb some simple lessons.

We should love the things we bring into our homes. When you carry in that old Windsor chair and carefully wax it, you give it new life. As it stands there in the living room glowing under the warmth of a lamp, born again, it reciprocates the attention, giving life back to you and your home. Sometimes I see a house or an apartment that hasn't been touched since the high-water moment when the family, decades before, was at its most expansive. When I find a room caught in this petrified mode, I know that household life has become routine; there's no sense that anything is going to happen that hasn't already happened. The oxygen has been depleted, and the rooms no longer entice you.

Although I've been designing for years, I've never felt more alive—more invested in the moment—than when decorating my own homes. From the time I signed the deeds, my senses were on high alert, even if I was just walking down the street. Shop windows, show houses, flea markets, and auction ads in the paper caught

First impressions count. This center hall, furnished with an English console table, American hooked rugs, and a French hall bench, sets a tone of elegance for a turn-of-the-century shingled house.

my eye. I had raised my family and was molting into a new shell. It was exhilarating to have new walls to conquer, more space to claim. I was curious about who I'd become and what I would look like reflected in my environment. Any house is a mirror.

I'm a practical person with an inquisitive eye and liberal taste buds. I like old, and I like new; I like Minimalism, and I like tradition. I love houses in Tuscany, with faded paint and velvet curtains, but I'm not willing to give up simplicity or to succumb to an opulence that encumbers my spirit. So I'm somewhere in the middle, not totally traditional and not quite contemporary. Besides, I don't want to be dominated by any one style. I believe in an eclectic mix.

A woman shopping for clothes knows the colors she likes and the lines that work for her. She buys a certain style. It's the same with a house: cultivate your intuition. The two years I spent fixing up my two new places amounted to a voyage of self-discovery. What do I like most about my life, and how can my rooms sustain that? What furniture do I want to keep? What do I want to take out of storage? How do I like to welcome my friends and my son and daughter into my home—how do rooms encourage our conversational intimacy? How does the house keep me company when I'm there by myself?

Good decorating is all about finding your own personal style. I'm constantly amazed that almost any interior or house can be made beautiful. There is no such thing as a sow's ear if you understand how to handle a space. Size is not an obstacle, not even if the ceilings are lobotomizingly low. (Actually, it's probably harder to work with grandeur than with modesty.) Every renovation, if it results in rooms with a sense of life and intelligence, is a tale with surprising turns. The story of my recent renovations may help you with your goals.

OVERLEAF
My collection of English drabware looks lovely in this corner cupboard, which is original to the house. I used a high-gloss finish on the cupboard to glorify its shell detailing. The hall chair is English, in its original paint.

I. My Own House

A House in the Country

THE DAY I DROVE with my broker into the driveway of my little saltbox in Remsenburg, New York, I loved it. The facade spoke to me. It was a 1790s shingled house in a historic district near other early houses—a little pocket of New England out there in eastern Long Island. The original rooms were really small, maybe twelve feet wide, and you couldn't fit more than three people in a room at any one time. At some point a kitchen had been built onto the back. The whole house was 2,500 square feet, if that—minus the steep staircase and the little corridor next to it. When I saw it, I could visualize what should happen: I could build on the charm.

The parkways to Connecticut and Long Island are paved with good intentions squandered on money-pits, and I couldn't afford for my little

LEFT

I think of this stately tree as God's umbrella, and it deserved a custom-made bench of its own.

OPPOSITE

A wrought-iron garden folly makes a shady retreat.

TOP
I turned the former chicken coop into a guest cottage.

ABOVE
Dogwood flanks the drive in the spring.

OPPOSITE
Here's my backyard, with the original house on the left and one new wing partly visible. The outbuildings on the right have become a laundry and more guest cottages.

country house to turn into Mr. Blanding's dream house. I had to be practical, and at times shrewd. (I won't bore you with the permit hassles. The process droned on for a year and a half, until my lawyer met with the chief building inspector and suggested that he probably didn't want a historic house in a historic district to fall apart while they all dotted the i's. There were holes in the roof, and the porch had become detached. I got my permit two weeks later.)

My new house was built like a kit ordered out of a Sears Roebuck catalog, I'm told, with numbered timbers holding it up, and small regular windows positioned straight across—the bedrooms upstairs had two little windows in the knee-wall under the eaves. Apparently in 1790, if you had small windows, you paid less in taxes. I don't know what they used for insulation then, but in some of the walls we found shredded paper, like the packing for bananas.

Beneath the encrustations the house wasn't quite Shaker, but it had a simple and straightforward Puritanical sensibility, like those slightly stiff faces in the journeyman portraits of the period. I thought the house was beautiful because of its purity, and if I wanted to keep it that way, I couldn't do too much. Design is always a matter of interpretation and judgment, especially in a project as sensitive as a house more than two centuries old. The terseness of the house, the fact that it said just one thing, and said it through compactness and plainness, steered my thoughts (while helping me contain the budget). The original front section was like a small red Monopoly house, and even though I needed to add a couple of rooms to make the house livable, I couldn't add too much without swamping its diminutive scale and contradicting the spare Colonial spirit. I had to know where to stop.

ADDING ON When you're adding on to a house, architects
and contractors are not a luxury but a necessity, because they're the
ones who can dependably get the materials and proportions right.
To work on my country home, I hired a local contractor, Eugen
Wons, and architect Mark Simon of Centerbrook Architects. I
asked Mark, with whom I'd collaborated before, to design a small
formal library on one side that would double as a dining room. (I
have not put a dining table there, but I like to have friends gather
on a sofa and a couple of chairs at a small table.) On the other side
I wanted to re-create the experience of a barn, with a room just tall
enough to feel two stories high. This would be the living room. In
this round of musical rooms, the old living room became the entry
and the keeping room became the center hall. After we completed
the plans, the heavy lifting began: the old house had to be raised so
that the floor could be made level and you could walk from room
to room without tripping. Lifting the structure allowed us to build
a crawl space and a real basement.
Formerly, the house sat on mud and a
few bricks.

Mark and I framed the original
house with two unequal additions,
because we didn't want to stiffen the
design with exact symmetries. We
preferred to imply that the house had
grown over time. Mark proportioned
the additions so that the original
core house set the stage for the whole
composition. Though we shingled the
additions to match the old centerpiece,
we varied details to distinguish them

After the construction was finished, the columns and side porch were painted to blend into the old house.

from the original. We chose triple-hung windows because they are tall enough to give you a great view, without windowsills to separate you from the outside. We could have created a similar effect with French doors, but with those you always have to be sure they're locked—windows seem a little less vulnerable. We hung tall shutters and painted them Essex green. The architects took care that the windows aligned and were correctly spaced so that all the elevations read properly from the exterior and interior. (We also ordered the windows way ahead of construction, to anticipate the long lead time.) The head of the local historical association, a neighbor, eyed the construction very carefully and was pleased that we didn't go overboard with something inflated. Our additions were respectful.

PRESERVING THE CHARACTER Restraint was the watchword inside as well. As a rule, you should never overdecorate anywhere, and especially not in a house that's pure and simple. You not only miss the head start you have when you build on its established character, but also risk sliding into pretension.

The charm that I fell in love with back on the driveway was really a kind of atmosphere stemming from age and fragility, and atmosphere in a house is always fragile, especially if you're adding rooms to an old structure. Fortunately, the few features the original house offered were still intact, and I could build on them. Even though each step of the steep old staircase reminded my body that this house was an antique, there was no way to redo it without losing a lot of space (and requiring more permits). A shallow brick hearth, probably once used for cooking, survived in one room. With its mellow patina, the hearth is a tapestry of time, and I kept the decor around it quiet. I left the wood mantel in this room natural, along with the wainscoting, and refreshed the white on the mantel and corner china cupboard in the other room.

I'm the type who wakes up in the middle of the night worrying. The big question that nagged me was how to carry over the atmosphere from the original house into the additions: How do you get the new stuff to look authentic? We did it with detail. We carried over to the new rooms the door trims and pilasters around the front entrance—they were simple, Greek revival, square-toothed moldings. To cut the crispness and get a softer edge on the new trim, I lavished four coats of white paint on it—two of the base coat and two of the cover. I'm a big believer in starting with a white house, and I use a

In this front hall, we balanced the simplicity and clean lines of a Shakeresque side table with an elaborately etched French mirror.

very soft white on the walls that isn't quite a cream—Donald Kaufman #5 to be exact. It's the perfect white, not hard-edged but pleasant. What people don't realize is that you can subtly vary the paint finishes to add another dimension to a room. If the trim is especially beautiful with finely carved details or lovely proportions, use paint with a higher sheen to make it sing. I painted the corner cupboards the same color as the walls, but in a semi-gloss rather than matte, and you can feel the difference.

Simple flooring is a powerful tool for setting the tone in a room—there's so much surface in your field of vision. To match the original wide-plank pine floors, my builder measured the size of the existing boards, had jigs made, and randomly laid planks, using varied

ABOVE

In the keeping room, I kept the original plain wood mantel
because it had an innate modesty that was part of the character
of the house. All I did was polish it. This room serves as a
center hall connecting the two new wings of the house, but it
also moonlights as a dining room when the table against the
wall is pulled out.

RIGHT

Around the French fruitwood farm table are the first set
of chairs I ever owned. I found them in the basement of an
antique shop on Third Avenue. The finials and backs are
slightly different on each pair. If I need to seat eight, the pair
of Heywood-Wakefield chairs on either side of the fireplace
are pressed into service.

I like a bathroom that feels more like a real room than a utilitarian space. One way to achieve that is to use a real piece of furniture, like this French server, as a vanity. I was able to keep one drawer by offsetting the sink. A stool, covered in a fragment of old Aubusson, slides underneath.

widths instead of standard measurements. We stained the wood to match the beautiful old honey color. All that surface area helped bring the character of the old house into the additions. Waxed floors are beautiful but require the kind of effort you don't really want to make in the country, so we opted for modern products that could duplicate the look of the old. We used a water-based polyurethane in a matte finish that doesn't look plastic. We laid a gray slate on the hearth and the face of the new architect-designed fireplaces.

The Puritanism that was so charming downstairs became a problem upstairs: the two small bedrooms shared a single, very modest bathroom. Not that I'm a card-carrying sybarite, but I do like to splash around. The library addition allowed me to add a master bedroom suite on the second floor and reconfigure the layout up there. I had a lot of fun figuring out how the new bathroom should work and look, and I finally decided that it should feel like a room, and that the vanity itself should be a wonderful old piece of furniture. I used the same pine flooring. The result is an up-to-date bathroom, but one that's not too aggressive for the house.

ARRANGING THE FURNITURE I have my own library of furniture squirreled away in storage, a collection of things I can't live without that are just waiting for a place to land. It's always a joy to go on a search for a new piece if there's a hole in a room, and my first stop is the garage. Choosing a piece from the collection of things I've tucked away is a little like having old friends over. It's very comforting. Furniture grouped in a room should feel like a family. If the pieces aren't right together, you'll never feel comfortable there. For Remsenburg, I decided to use traditional, formal pieces, and so I bypassed my stash of painted country pieces in favor of more elegant furniture inspired by eighteenth-century drawing rooms.

Decorating the walls comes last, and they make a big difference. In the entry off the side porch, I thought I'd hang a mirror, but it looked flat. I replaced it with a portrait I'd planned to use over the fireplace in the living room but needed here. In the living room I hung a portrait of a boy who looks like he might have

In the library, I decided I needed a new color in my life, so I added a red-and-white striped chair, on casters for flexibility. The English sofa and storage box—perfect as a coffee table—came already upholstered in red floral damask. The three bold patterns work in this room because the colors are the same.

The square columns on the new side porch were copied from the original pilasters on the front of the house, and the bead-board fits right in with the rustic style. I love the sculptural quality of the wire bench and set it next to a little green table I spotted at a junk shop. I found the lanterns on sale in a Pottery Barn catalog and bought a dozen.

come over on the *Mayflower*. It was an intuitive move, and I was amazed when I did it because he looked as if he'd always been there. Every time I walk into those rooms I get excited. You have to break the symmetry of a room, and your old ways of thinking, to make it come alive. I'm not interested in rules so much as in the life being created, even when you're working with historical furnishings.

When you're in a room alone, you need a little company, and since I'm often in the country by myself, I put a television in practically every room—it's taken the place of a radio. But you don't want to over-technologize a room. The television in the library is teeny and tucked unobtrusively on a shelf. I also have one in the kitchen for watching the cooking shows—we all love those channels. There's a small television in the sunroom for catching a favorite program. The living room gets the large television, for watching movies.

I've set the house up for activities, not just entertaining. I also managed to find a little place on the way to the attic, a spot used for storage, to put my old French drawing board. I do my watercolors there under a beautiful window that gives the most serene light.

Building something for yourself is a long process, but a compelling one that takes you back to the basics, starting with foundations. The process of building these additions helped me understand the house beyond its surfaces and finishes. Through renovation, my tired old house gradually became more interesting. The

original was reframed by something new, and revalued. But even within this expanded context, I understood that details—like extending the classical molding to the new additions, and taking the flat pilasters from the front porch to the side porch—made the difference and brought the house to life. By the end, I was exhausted but refreshed. I felt, finally, that I too was reborn along with the house.

A master stonemason constructed the new chimney with an applied panel of chevron brickwork, made from antique bricks.

An Apartment in the City

OPPOSITE

Pre-war buildings in
New York are laden with
character. I'm always
spotting something that
I never noticed before,
like the beautifully carved
arabesque on this lintel.

OVERLEAF

My New York living room
is filled with with favorite
pieces of furniture
accumulated over the
years. The sofa has a
high arm,which makes it
extremely comfortable to
sit in. The French bergère
covered in its original
embossed velvet is my
reading chair. The coffee
table is a classic Billy
Baldwin design.

MEANWHILE, back in Manhattan, it was time to move. Maybe I was crazy to take on a second project at the same time, but I had to vacate my old apartment because the lease was up. Doing two houses at once was a little like caring for twins—you love them both and just forge ahead.

I looked and looked and then bought a seven-room apartment reminiscent of my old 1920s apartment, not merely out of nostalgia. Like many people, I feel more comfortable in an older building with high ceilings, thick walls, masonry fireplaces, and mantels with character. I look for good volume, which means a satisfying sense of space with an intimate, even cozy feel. Spaces compose people psychologically. Brownstones, for example, with their rooms front and back, help contain family life and make everyone feel part of a unit.

The apartment I found was a tad deficient in the trim and moldings department. I love Minimalism, but apartments that are plain don't appeal to me. Happiness is when my eye settles on the subtly curved edges of a raised panel door or glances up to a fixture on a ceiling that splashes light. Any element in a room might give me pleasure, even everyday, ordinary things. In a cold, cost-consciously designed apartment, however, you have to work at conjuring character. It certainly can be done, but you're starting at a deficit.

Apartments in any city have built-in pros and cons, so you have to reconnoiter a bit before knowing what's up. Study the

geographical basics—where are the prevailing breezes, noise patterns, and views? I was careful to buy an apartment located in the rear of the building because in the city that location is quieter. If you live facing the street, you're usually looking straight at the facade opposite.

You have to open your senses when you scout. What makes a room joyous is the quality of the light. I want light and sky and air and freshness in every room. When you're walking through a prospective apartment, try to visualize whether you could spend the holidays there. Even the approach to the front door matters. The lobby in my new building was standard-issue but nicely appointed, and it was small enough to create a level of intimacy.

CONSOLIDATING SPACE When it comes to creating spaces, some people are afraid of touching walls. They consider them immovable. For me, the floor plan is always negotiable. But because I found an apartment with spatial qualities that I liked, it didn't make sense to shuffle walls. I kept the basic configuration of the seven-room apartment and left the pipes where they were. Old buildings are crotchety, and when you start meddling with their water systems you can open yourself up to a lot of problems. Instead, I surgically altered a few wall areas in the new place. I borrowed a bit of space from the maid's room to enlarge the bath, and I created a wall pocket for the Sub-Zero in the kitchen.

The kitchen is always the comfort zone in a house, the place where you can really hang out. Mine is gloriously square, unlike many in New York that have been gerrymandered from a previous layout of servants' quarters and storage closets. There's a great big sunny window suitable as a breakfast area. It's the first place I go both in the morning and when I come home—and not just when I need a snack.

The most expensive space in a house to renovate is usually the kitchen. If you're judicious in your plans, you can save a lot of money and still make a big difference. I decided to leave the kitchen pretty much as it was. Instead of changing all the cabinets, I spruced them up with sturdier hinges, new pulls, and better lighting. I replaced the green Formica countertops with stainless steel, which instantly gave the room a clean, professional feel. Stainless steel is a great alternative because it's virtually indestructible. You have to worry about food stains with many granites and especially marbles, which are generally more porous. Miracle products like Corian, a plastic composite, can be more expensive than granite. You can also get counters with integrated sinks and a running backsplash done at kitchen fabricators, such as Home Depot and Ikea, for reasonable prices.

MAKING THE MOST OF WHAT'S THERE

An empty room is like a blank canvas, but before you make your first stroke, you have to assess what's already there. Often the room is a mess, with too many light switches whose placement hasn't been thought out and smoke detectors that should be repositioned out of sight. In my apartment I spent a lot of time tidying up the shell, reorganizing details, and clearing away the unnecessary accessories. I started with the ceiling and worked my way down the walls.

When I clear out a room, it's usually easy to find its flaws—an awkward shape, ill-proportioned windows in need of camouflage, inadequate lighting. Cleaning up the shell of my apartment allowed me to see that I should replace all the doors, to give the

If I have a flat surface, I instinctively create a tablescape. Here I've gathered a Calder-esque mobile, an Aesthetic Movement vase, and a Chinese pot on two nineteenth-century Chinese work tables pulled next to each other. A Robert Motherwell drawing hangs above and completes the composition.

apartment uniformity down to the hinges. Doors make a huge difference in an apartment, and not merely because good doors close and lock better. Walking through a space and opening and closing good heavy doors lifts your whole impression of the apartment. I chose solid doors with panel details. Then I picked out antique nickel for the hardware. Brass, to me, stops the eye, so I went with the beautifully muted white metal that was so popular in the 1920s and 1930s. Its subtle luster quietly animates a room.

You can fix a room's lighting only if you're already pulling the place apart. Since I was reworking some of the walls, I used the opportunity to install recessed mini-lights in the bedroom hall to display my favorite pictures. This allowed me to clean up a ceiling that had some awkward beams and fixtures.

Floors really matter, and I usually leave them bare. Luckily my floors were in good condition, so I could avoid refinishing them and eliminating their hard-won character. I replaced some of the worn strips and ran the hardwood into the bathrooms. Instantly they started to look like rooms. When I did the bathroom walls, I avoided the typical ceramic tiles by working out a formula for cutting up marble squares to get two large rectangles and three smaller squares from a single twelve-by-twelve tile. We laid them in a running bond, using the larger pieces on the master bathroom walls and the smaller ones on the walls in the guest bathroom.

Some old buildings have drop-dead beautiful moldings, but after they've been painted over for decades they lose their detail. Moreover, with decades of different

OPPOSITE

Any bookcase will look better if you tuck a few talismans in among the books. I love the little painting by Jim Sullivan and propped it beside two Egyptian wooden figures and a casual pile of amber beads and African stamps.

BELOW

The toile on the armchair picks up the same blue-and-white that's in the tattersall silk taffeta curtains hanging at my bedroom windows. An English Regency clothespress hides the TV.

owners, an apartment often has a hodgepodge of moldings that don't match. It's easiest to take off tired moldings and replace them with something similar. I pulled all the moldings off and started over so that their profiles would be crisp.

DOUBLE-DUTY ROOMS In my old apartment we rarely went into the living room. Since then, I've learned to diversify a room so that it serves dual purposes, whether it's watching a film and reading, or visiting with friends and catching up on some work. People complete rooms with their activities.

I read and work in every room of my home, so I tried to adapt each for a double function. Books are such an important part of my life that I can't live in a room without shelves. I found pine bookcases in an antique shop and used them to line one wall of the living room so that I could reach up, take down a book, and sit on a chair positioned next to the fire. Early in the morning I'm more likely to be at the oval table in the dining room. I often read and work in my bedroom, which is like a junior suite in a hotel. To catch light from both ends of the building, I connected the master bedroom and guest bedroom, which I use as a small office and sitting room. I bought a Swedish daybed for the guestroom so that it can accommodate both work and the occasional guest.

Of course, the moment of truth comes when you're arranging the furniture. Since I wanted the apartment to stay light and open, I decided there wouldn't be a lot. The scale of the rooms couldn't take too many pieces, but I placed a small sofa and three club chairs in the living room, along with two ample, very comfortable armchairs. A big sofa that's been in my life for twenty years went into the dining room.

I have no skirts on any of the furniture, so air and light flow in the space beneath them. The pieces themselves are simple and classic in their lines, but they're not all one style. They're English, French, Italian, American, and Spanish, but they talk to each other. Each has an individual twist, yet they defer to the ensemble. I tried, as always, for a harmonious whole.

I believe that architecture and decoration are art forms of the highest order—and that includes everything from furniture to molding to fabric. On the following pages, I'll go back to the beginning and lead you step by step through the various stages of my decorating process. I'll show you how to bring out the best features of a room, how to arrange furniture so that conversation flows, and how to finish it off with the right details. Come with me antiquing for the perfect chair, and I'll tell you what I look for in a leg. I'll walk you through a range of styles, and then I'll show you how to mix it all up. When you're building a room, you're building character, and character is the strength and wisdom of a home.

My eighteenth-century Spanish painted and gilded headboard may not be the most comfortable thing in the world, but I adore it, and it has followed me from house to house. One of Donald Kaufman's chameleon colors is on the walls—a cream with a slight blush. It changes as the light shifts during the day.

2. GETTING STARTED

*Details are what the eye
fastens on and remembers.*

YOU'RE ON A RECONNAISSANCE MISSION when you walk into a room that you're about to decorate. Before you even pick up a paintbrush, you have to figure out how the room should work. It's a matter of fact-finding. Notice how you enter, and how you exit. Is the door in the right place? What's the shape of the room? The height? Where does the light come in? What about the proportions of the windows? Are there any views? Knowing the basics will not only give you a sense of how the room should work but also suggest its character: What does the room want to be? If the windows are tall and thin, you could play into the elegant verticality and cultivate a sophisticated uptown look. A low ceiling might connote the intimacy of a cottage or the flowing lines of a modern interior. A lot of what you do in putting a room together is common

PAGES 32–33

The white walls and dark
woodwork in this entrance
foyer, designed by Robert
A. M. Stern Architects,
are so beautiful that the
space speaks for itself.

OPPOSITE

In this bathroom, the
washing-up area is
separated from the bathing
area by a pair of French
doors. The glass doors allow
both light and intimacy.

LEFT

Against the cool white shell
of my little entrance hall,
every piece of furniture
stands out. I like the fact
that the English Gothic
lantern is overscaled. It
makes a dramatic statement
as soon as you walk in. The
Danish painted pine table
is very versatile—it's
actually two half-rounds
that make a whole.

sense, not magic—a matter of building on the givens and designing to its strengths.

I love the clarity of uncurtained windows and doors. Nothing gets in the way of the sunlight streaming in on the polished wood floors and the Claes Oldenburg eraser.

If you have the luxury of a fresh start because you've recently moved in or have just thrown everything out, it's better to tinker with the room while it's still empty. Clean up the lines so it reads as a simple volume of space. In a bare room you can better assess all the fixtures without being swayed by the furnishings and fabrics. It's easier to spot flaws when a room is stripped, and much harder to make corrective moves later with just furniture and paint. You'll sail along if you first do the prep work.

CLEANING UP THE SHELL

An architect builds a house on foundations. Your basic building block is the shell—a room's walls, floor, and ceiling. You have to be able to see a room clearly to understand how it will support your design. In terms of its physical footprint or visual integrity, the shell may have to be changed. It's usually a good idea to remove unnecessary additions—intruding cabinets or closets, mismatched moldings, and unwanted valances—to take a room back to its original, pure state. Or you can add details to strengthen the shell. If there's an intrusion in the space, you might want to integrate it into the room by building its companion. For example, if you have a closet at one end, add another one at the other end to make a symmetrical pair. This is the time to be disciplined as you distill a notion of the room's basic character and edit and make amends.

What do you want the shell to do? Break up the room in your mind to analyze how the parts come together. If you're lucky enough to have a room with architectural features, start thinking about how to emphasize and enhance them. A fireplace or an alcove can become the focal point of the room. If you live in an older house, there may be moldings or even a plaster rosette in the middle of a ceiling that you'll probably want to bring out. Moldings are the equivalent of line drawings in space, and when deployed creatively they can correct proportions—turning squat rooms tall, for example.

Even if your rooms aren't antebellum wonders, the shell will still be an important part of a room. The foundations you're building on

The finished living room
has a big barnlike interior,
with no boundary between
the walls and the ceiling,
so I painted them all the
same color. The carpet has
no sharp color turns and
blurs into the floor. What
makes the Albrizzi iron-
and-glass coffee table from
the 1960s so wonderful is
that it's so elusive—you
see right through it. I hung
the painting low to the
fireplace to maintain a
sense of intimacy with
the furniture grouping.

When I first saw this nineteenth-century barn, it was about to fall down, but the forms were so beautiful that I had to rescue it. We cleaned it, fixed it, and painted the huge volume all white. The fireplace we designed was originally very plain, but when I found a painted wood overdoor and made legs for it, it became a mantel. I carefully considered every object I brought in because I didn't want to spoil the purity.

are the walls, ceiling, and floor, and you can't ignore these background elements. Assess the quantity and quality of floor and wall space, and note the location of openings like doors and windows. If you tidy up the planes of a room, the volume emerges as a feature in itself.

It's relatively easy to see what's wrong with the picture when you walk into a room—an awkward layout, ill-proportioned windows, inadequate light. The real trick is to figure out how to turn each negative into a positive. Even the contractor-built houses that most of us live in can acquire bones. You needn't accept bland. Build a savings account of details in your memory bank that you can draw from by visiting your local lumberyard, skimming through catalogs, dropping in at historic house museums, frequenting decorator show houses, or clipping pictures of rooms you like from magazines. Of course, simplicity itself might be the answer, and you may decide to eliminate moldings and baseboards in favor of a hard modernist edge. The idea is to start building character with the shell.

CEILINGS Don't overdo the ceiling: you want the eye to stay at the level of the furniture and paintings. If you have beams in your ceilings, sometimes it's advantageous to add an extra one to match existing beams and create a rhythmic pattern that contributes to a sense of symmetry and balance. People often paint a ceiling the same color as the walls, because a contrasting color can stop the eye and put a lid on the room. Still, that doesn't mean walls and ceilings have to be exactly the same shade. It's usually more interesting to make the ceilings slightly darker or lighter. I often tint it pale pink, peach, or vanilla: a blush of color adds mood to a room.

WALLS Walls deserve more care than you would initially think. Unless you're dealing with an old Spanish Colonial house with expressive trowel marks on the plaster or a Victorian with vestiges of color that hint of an intriguing past, smooth out the imperfections. Usually a good painter can handle the normal cracks and blemishes. But in apartments encrusted with decades of paint, I've often found that a skim coat of plaster is just what's needed to give me a spanking clean shell. A long run of flawless wall space is the best frame for your pictures.

When it comes to light switches and outlets, absence makes the eye grow fonder. Be ruthless. Electricians like to see their handiwork. I don't. Though you may need a contractor, you don't have to be an architect to give your walls a face-lift. Tuck the plugs around a corner out of sight, and gang the switches in a neat, continuous row, hiding them too if possible. Likewise with air registers, which should be neither seen nor heard. If given the choice, I prefer to put an air vent on the floor rather than in a wall, but engineers have gotten very clever recently in designing diffusers that can slip in alongside moldings almost undetected, like shadowy reveals.

Most of us are working with eight-foot-tall ceilings and twelve-foot-high aspirations. There are several techniques that will help you create the illusion of greater height. Light colors, which tend to expand a room, lend it greater height as well, especially if you carry the color, or its near match, onto the ceiling. You can also lift the height of a room with the age-old trick of accentuating the vertical lines. Pick out the trim around doorways and windows in a color that contrasts slightly with the surrounding walls. For example, a bright white against a cream will subtly give a vertical thrust to a space.

Upstairs, I tucked the bed right under the eaves and painted the walls and ceiling white so that they would read as pure form. The circular headboard is another Spanish painted piece, and I love to juxtapose it with an early American quilt, inset with a white square. Many people assume a regular table is too high to put beside a bed, but these French fruitwood tables work just fine. Hansen swing-arm lamps are perfect for reading in bed.

BELOW

The big, wide, floor-to-ceiling windows in the sunroom were custom-made with a bold grid. I fitted them with solar-screen shades to make it easier to read there, even in bright sunlight.

OPPOSITE

I added more wood to the dining room doorway and finished it to match the living room bookcase. These rooms work almost as one unit. Parties spill over from one to the other, so each needs comfortable seating. I don't like those dead, unused dining rooms with just a big empty table in the middle.

DOORS AND WINDOWS The entrance of a home is important. Your hands are always opening and closing doors, and solid-core doors telegraph that the house is sturdy. There's something satisfying about the *whoosh* that's made when a tightly fitted, beautifully crafted door closes on a cushion of air. Guests will remember lifting a big brass knocker at a mahogany front door with raised panels. Inside, doors are just as important. In a contemporary house, smooth doors that almost vanish into the walls contribute to the seamless, streamlined effect. You're guilty of mixing metaphors when you combine flush and raised-panel doors in the same room. Keep the doorways at the same height, and the trim the same all around. An exception to the rule should be exceptional, something you really want to feature.

Doors are generally easier than you think to change, and customizing an opening gives you a lot of look for the money. You might want to take a door all the way up to the ceiling to usher in more light and create a better spatial flow. You can do this by

putting in a new doorjamb and buying a custom door. Or you can double the width of the doorjamb to create enough room for a pair of French doors, which gives a room a greater sense of ceremony and procession. Maybe you don't even require a door in the larger opening. If your style is traditional, celebrate whatever move you make with strong moldings that confirm the geometry. If it's a feeling of age you're after, recycle an antique door.

If it's in your budget and the floor plan, start setting up symmetries in a room by aligning doorways, centering openings within walls, or ganging windows in a row to form a group. Lining up doors between rooms in what the French call an enfilade is an old trick for giving a house sweep and grandeur.

Sliding glass doors are especially hard to deal with. Don't put vertical blinds on them, because that only aggravates the problem. If possible, replace the sliders with French doors, either contemporary or traditional, depending on the style of the house and

LEFT

The height of this double-story dining room dictated a fixture of equal stature. This early American iron chandelier measured up.

OPPOSITE

The two rows of twenty-four-inch-square stacked windows are based on the barn's original fenestration, reinterpreted by architect Raymond Gomez. The room is twenty feet high, and the immense wall would have been too imposing if we had not broken it up with light.

the interiors. French doors actually give you full openness, jamb to jamb, as opposed to the half you get when sliding doors are open. If you have wall space next to the sliding doors, a quick trick is simply to frame them with a soft fabric to take off that hard edge.

Big picture windows were a 1950s thing, and if you inherited them with the house, you can mitigate their impact in several ways. Side panels will diminish the size of the glass, depending on their width. If you have a lovely view, then go with your picture window, bearing in mind, however, that these windows sometimes drain the energy of a room and at night they go black, chilling the space.

I keep window dressings minimal to bring out the architectural impact of windows and trim. But curtains and valances can come in very handy when you have to correct discrepancies in height and even up the tops of mismatched windows. A consistent horizontal line helps confer tranquillity on a space.

The vaguely Anglo-Indian
slat-back chairs are from my
own line of furniture. The
split-wood rocker is a classic
from the Adirondacks. I use
this Shaker bookcase, built
in three parts, as architecture
or art, forgetting its more
prosaic purpose. Instead
of books, it holds a small
collection of miniature
chairs. Some people have
a fetish for shoes; I have a
fetish for chairs. A child's
wooden hoop from the
1800s rests on top.

FLOORS The bedroom is the only room in the house that virtually dictates wall-to-wall carpets: the softness gives a sense of intimacy, especially if the color of the wall extends to the color of the carpet and creates a virtual cocoon. Besides, there's something nice and tactile about padding around in your bare feet on a cut-pile carpet (and vacuuming is a breeze).

Elsewhere you can use a big carpet to stretch the dimensions of the floor and make a small room look bigger. Leave a little bit of the wood showing: a wide expanse of rug gathers the furniture into a group, and the wooden floor edges the room like a frame, bringing everything into a neat geometry. You can get away with a large inexpensive rug, like sisal, if you add a distinctive border, such as a black cotton trim. The look is graphic and gives the room a sophisticated snap.

In bigger rooms, large rugs can be boring because of the monotony of the exposed surface. Use one or more area rugs to help define seating areas. Think of area rugs as visual support for the furniture groupings: if they have patterns, they shouldn't shout and compete with the upholstery.

LEFT
On weekends I like to do watercolors at the table by the window in the library.
OPPOSITE
A farmhouse table would have been a little too obvious, so I furnished the kitchen with a neoclassical table painted bright orange and surrounded it with faux-bois painted metal, Regency-style garden chairs.

There are so many synthetic woods these days that a so-called wood floor no longer guarantees you a sense of quality. My eye always savors the inlaid patterns you find in old floors. That level of craft today is rare—but not impossible. There's no reason why you can't lay old white or red oak into an interesting pattern in a foyer, for example. Blond floors, like the increasingly popular maple, give the consistency of a fine complexion to a room, and recycled flooring adds the depth of age that you don't get with newly milled products.

The style you are beginning to envision for the space, along with the color of your furniture, will help you choose the color of the floor. An ebony stain for contemporary spaces looks smart, but many people prefer staining, or pickling, the floors to a light shade, which dematerializes the surfaces and relaxes the pull of gravity on the furniture. Everything lightens up. For a more country look, use a natural finish. Rich red-browns are what we associate with traditional furniture. Recently there's been a trend toward leaving wood floors, even softwood floors, unfinished. The idea comes out of old Swiss and Scandinavian buildings, including grand Danish palaces. The natural look is disarming, but be ready to mop.

At the other end of the color—and conceptual—spectrum are aniline dyes, which are used to make colored varnishes. If you've decided to make artificiality into an aesthetic, you've entered a free zone and are behaving and misbehaving by your own rules. This high-risk route is for the brave. I've seen some startling watery-blue floors, but you may tire of the self-centered colors.

You should also take care with the degree of gloss. You don't want your floor to look like a basketball court (unless your ceiling is so low that you need five coats of urethane to give you depth from the reflections). I prefer a more subtle finish, usually matte,

In the barn I kept the floors bare, to be cool underfoot in summer.

52

ROOMS

but nothing shinier than satin, which resists the glare of bulbs and keeps a room visually quiet by absorbing rather than bouncing light. Beeswax is incredibly elegant, especially as it develops a patina (and squeak) over time. But it commits you, or someone you're paying, to a lifetime of hard labor, so think twice.

Some people want everything to be polished and perfect, including the floor, but to me that level of finish implies a house that isn't being used (and certainly not by kids). In highly trafficked rooms I don't try for a highly polished look since the imperfections that naturally come from use stand out.

MOLDINGS In a traditional space, moldings are a gift. They possess a tremendous power of visual connotation, their lines can stretch space and their profiles can create a sense of substance and style. But they can be anemic if not appropriately scaled. Make sure they fit the proportions of the room. A twelve-foot ceiling can easily support twelve-inch crown moldings; an eight-foot ceiling would get only a six-inch molding. Plaster crowns are much better than wood, which sometimes separates from the ceiling. If the ceiling is high enough, you can add chair rails for instant character.

The quickest fix is beefing up the baseboards. A four-inch baseboard, for example, is token, and you could take it up to six or nine inches—and if the ceiling is very high, even up to eleven inches. Baseboards, chair rails, and crown moldings emphasize the horizontal belt around a room, especially when they're highlighted in white or a color that contrasts slightly with the walls. The sum total of these banding gestures helps contain and focus a space so that you have the sense of a "there" there when you're finally sitting in the room.

Retaining the banister, hardware, and moldings preserved the original character of this shingled house.

DETAILS
COUNT

Details, such as wall
finishes and hardware,
help accessorize a room
and tie a look together.
Strive to establish a
consistent tone from the
very beginning, making
sure that each successive
decision agrees with the previous one while anticipating the next.
Achieving the same level of quality from the shell down to the
doorknobs helps create this consistency: an agreement of parts all
along the way adds up to a harmonious whole.

Using quality materials is fundamental in elevating the tone of
a room. Begin with a good bucket of paint beautifully applied: the
roller should have the right nap, and brushes should be specific to
the task. I think it pays to bring in a professional, who will start the
interior off right with a tight application.

From the time you first shake hands with the front doorknob,
you're subliminally forming an opinion of a space. Details are the
equivalent of jewelry. Heavy hardware—doorknobs, hinges, locks—
is like silver at the dinner table: it adds a tangible elegance to a
room. Once there was only a choice of chrome or brass finishes,
but now you can choose brushed chrome, brushed brass, gilded

ABOVE

I hung an antique lace
valance at the window.

OPPOSITE

The leaf-print pillows on
the pair of English club
chairs were left over from
a show house.

brass, nickel, or antique nickel. I've always found brass rather loud—brassy, actually. English rooms can carry it off because they usually have a lot of color. But most modern architects prefer brushed stainless steel: white metals convey a sense of modernity, while yellow implies tradition. If you wanted a sense of age fifty years ago, you recycled old hardware. Now you don't have to, because catalogs have a long historical memory. And don't forget hinges. They can add a little shine to the quality of the space.

Hardware is convincing to the touch when it's hefty rather than hollow. Shapes too make a difference. Consider oval or even mushroom knobs. Lever handles can vary from straight modernist rods to those with a traditional bent. English levers can look like Sheffield silver and are suitable for a library; French ones are more florid and flamboyant, perfect on a pair of doors that open onto a terrace.

The authenticity of your room starts at the shell. The days of true plaster walls are over in all but the most expensive construction. Most contractors now use gypsum board, which is hollow in comparison. You can overcome that by using thicker widths, or even doubling it up between bedrooms by backing it with plywood. Applying a thin coat of plaster over Sheetrock is the closest we come to the good old days of real plaster. If you go this route, you can impregnate the plaster with pigment, which will give the walls an appealing patina and the visual rhythm of the craftsman's hand. This is a variation of an old Italian technique, called stucco Veneziano, which involves stirring dry pigment into wet plaster. It creates a mottled finish and guarantees an instant sense of age.

You're way ahead in the authenticity department if you judiciously use a few architectural antiques in your house. The classic retrofit is a marble mantelpiece plucked from Europe,

but you can find doors, windows, period chandeliers, and many other pieces at specialized emporiums, architectural salvage stores, junk shops, or yard sales.

Details are what the eye fastens on and remembers. One significant detail, such as an antique mantel, can carry an entire room. It can make a new house feel as if it has a history and put the soul back into an old space.

Recycling also applies to design. An architectural artifact like this old attic window brings in more light and adds some character to an upstairs bedroom in this renovated barn.

3. The Big Picture

Some people throw furniture around a room freely, but Einstein said, "God doesn't play dice with the universe," and I don't think you should play dice with a room.

NOW THAT YOU'VE CLEANED UP your space and you can see the architectural shell clearly—with its doorways, windows, bare floors, and blank walls—you may be tempted to go out shopping. But not yet. Hold on. Contain your enthusiasm. You need an idea for the room, a concept of how you're going to live there, and what you're really going to need. A furniture plan. Invest in a little tracing paper before investing in a new chaise longue. Take heart when you stare at the blank sheets: at most, there are only three good layouts for any one space.

The ABCs of drawing up a plan are simple and actually fun, like constructing a puzzle in space. Get someone to hold the end of a measuring tape while you take the dimensions of each room. Then scale the dimensions down and draw the room's outline on a pad, noting the placement of doors, windows, fireplace, and so on. For convenience,

I often use gridded drawing paper, on which each quarter-inch square represents a square foot. Stand in a corner and take photographs, ratcheting the camera slowly from left to right to get all four walls. Then tape the photos into a composite panorama. You're putting together the working documents that will be the basis of your thoughts and scribblings. As you're setting down the facts, you're casing the joint, trying to understand its subtleties and secrets. Does any feature, like a fireplace or skylight, stand out? What do you see when you first walk in? Do the photos reveal anything about the proportions—a low ceiling in a wide room or window frames that could use a little beefing up? The plan of the existing space and the photographs give you an overview that allows you to think of the architecture as an opportunity waiting for you to come in with all your powers of invention.

PAGES 60–61
I like to place the bed near a window.

OPPOSITE
Sunlight pours into the corner of this large living room, and I didn't want to waste it. I created a conversational group with the chairs. A Spanish rug defines the area. Even in winter it feels like a rose garden.

LEFT
The beginnings of a project: the conference room table covered with plans.

Get a Fix on Function

You should ask yourself two simultaneous questions, and the answers should eventually come together in your plan: What do *you* want the room to be, and what does *it* want to be?

Most people have some grasp of the functional issues right away. I always ask myself what a room will be used for: eating, sleeping, reading, paying bills, or watching television? Make a list of your needs. Just what would you like to do in this room? Will you be entertaining every other week in the living room, or will it be mostly solitaire? Will the dining room be formal or casual? How many people do you expect to accommodate in each space—two, eight, or twelve? Or is it a space where nobody stays very long, such as a hall, gallery, or vestibule? Do you need a place to put your drink down? A lamp to read by? A stool to put your feet on? Do you want to look at a view? Sit in front of the fire? Either mentally or on paper, establish the

OPPOSITE
This dressing room doubles as an exercise space. Mirrored closet doors let you check out your posture, and you should always have a comfortable place to sit while you pull on your socks.

LEFT
I made myself an elegant master bath with mahogany wainscoting, a marble-topped vanity, and a china sink. The lever-handled faucet in a nickel finish is a perennial favorite. I put the marble inside the shower, not on the walls, which are hung with photographs by Richard Avedon and others.

program. Don't forget to think about how you enter the room, leave it, and circulate inside it in the meantime.

Programming the rooms is the first of your many chances to think outside the box. You can make the function of a room multiple and expand your space without annexing a single square foot—the dining room doubles as a library, the den converts into a guest room, or the bedroom functions as a home office.

Don't think of your plan merely as the sum of all the requirements. There should be a vision behind it. Vision, in this case, is more than a matter of choosing a sophisticated French Empire style, say, over American country. Are the spatial assumptions behind the plan modern, with each piece of furniture floating in a generous amount of space? Or is your concept traditional, with layers of objects clustered into denser groups? Is that same bowl of space half empty or half full?

Many of my rooms look traditional because of the antiques and the symmetries, but I'm really a closet modernist. And I think most people these days are, whether or not they know it. I like to surround each piece with enough space to let it breathe. I move furniture toward the room's center, where the forms can be seen from all sides. This puts an added burden on me as a designer to choose furniture with strong sculptural lines. The architecture becomes a backdrop to the furniture rather than having to carry the whole room.

Any function can be accommodated in the process of drawing up your plan, and sooner or later your intuitions and taste enter the equation. Unless you're creating formal period rooms, you have to discover your own style. Should this particular room be dramatic or quiet, intimate or grand? If it has a garden exit, should you try to capture a sense of the out-of-doors, or do you prefer to think of it as a haven from nature?

66
❖
ROOMS

You can always turn to texture to create a more interesting room. In a Washington, D.C., home, I used rag rugs to dress up the small hall. The faux-bois paint on the American chest of drawers adds more texture, and more color comes in with the painted Windsor chair.

My living room in London is the
quintessential multipurpose space.
I can work, eat, relax, or entertain in
this room. I put old English limestone
pilasters on either side of the window
to dramatize the twelve-foot-high ceiling.
The painted Gothic bookcase fits in
stylistically with the tracery ceiling.

OPPOSITE

Three mirrors, including the gilt
Regency square over the fireplace,
enhance the impression of space.
I designed the massive mahogany
mantel to suit the room's large scale.

RIGHT

A pair of comfortable chairs flank an
octagonal table.

I usually start visualizing
the kind of furniture I want
in a room as soon as I walk
in, and I know what it should
look like fairly quickly. When you're doing your own house,
however, you naturally think of the furniture you already own. You
have to take stock and pencil in the pieces you want to keep. Start
with the largest items, such as sofas, pianos, tables, and bookcases.
Then count off the feet on your grid drawing and start positioning
the furniture with a more realistic sense of its fit and location. Cut
out pieces to represent your chairs and sofa (measure them too)
and start moving them around. The grids make it easier not only
to establish the furniture groupings but also to keep track of the
passages in between, where there has to be room to walk. Be very
careful to allow enough space without wasting it.

A writing table behind the
sofa catches the morning light.

OPPOSITE

A tapestry-covered stool
offers additional seating.

THE ARCHITECTURAL
ARRANGEMENT OF FURNITURE

Other decorators might start with a great fabric, or a fabulous carpet, but I believe in beginning with the fundamentals. At heart I'm a geometrician, and I trust in furniture plans. If the structure of the design—that is, the placement of the furniture and the flow around it—isn't right, I don't care how beautiful the fabric and rug are, the room is going to fail. So I start with the plan and proceed to the more colorful parts of the design in an ordered progression.

Some people throw furniture around a room freely, but as Einstein said, "God doesn't play dice with the universe," and I don't think you should play dice with a room. It drives me crazy when I see furniture used like wallpaper, when people fill a room with stuff without any regard for the bones. I personally find my sanity in arranging ordered constellations of furniture, even if the chairs, tables, and sofas are from different countries and periods. The harmony comes from the carefully calibrated relationship of one object to another.

I try to arrange rooms in which each piece of furniture shows respect for the others. It's what architects call the ordination of parts. I pay particular attention to how the furniture and the room relate. When a room doesn't come with good architectural features, I might use a pair of boldly shaped chairs to lend it structure and then anchor the chairs by using them to bracket a fireplace.

I may be the only one who thinks of my rooms as radical, but what is quietly subversive about my arrangements is that I often pull pieces off the wall to create islands of furniture, sometimes on an area rug. Rather than hugging a room's perimeter, the sofas and chairs are arranged to float in the space, toward the center, in intimate clusters intended to focus conversation. And instead of creating one

I didn't want to gussy up the simple wrought-iron frame with a canopy or a bedskirt. The dark picture frames echo the dark iron.

all-or-nothing central seating area that marginalizes the perimeter, I prefer to create two, or even more, symmetrical groups. You need to keep conversational groupings small because you can't physically talk to eight people across too much space.

A bedroom can also be conducive to conversation as long as you provide enough seating. If space permits, a small sofa could be a place to read the newspaper or talk over the day's schedule as your mate puts on his or her shoes. A bench at the foot of the bed is a

great spot to pack a suitcase. (It can also hold the bedspread while you sleep.) I often put a slipper chair, or a pair of chairs, in a bedroom so that clients have a convenient place to perch in the morning while dressing or at night while getting ready for bed.

I think there is a geometry to conversation, and the secret is in keeping people close and facing each other. When I come into a room and hear chatter, I know the dimensions are working and the plan is succeeding.

4. Supporting Elements

Composing a room is like writing music—
you need exciting passages, and then moments
to rest your eye.

MY CARDINAL RULE is to build a room around its geometries. You can't go wrong if you find the central axis, cross-axis, or center of a space and construct conversational groups around it. For example, a centerline drawn from the fireplace might suggest an axis for other seating areas, each with its own orbit of influence in the geography of the room. The axes naturally map out the traffic patterns—they follow the entries into a room, the paths through it, and the borders around it. I try to make the circulation bypass the seating clusters and leave them intact as places of rest in undisturbed pools of spatial quiet. The furniture arrangement creates processional passages, and the flow should continue from one room to the next and the next.

You always have to remember the relationship of one room to another. What

will you see when you look through the doorway? Often you can coordinate the plans of adjoining rooms to continue an axis and create a larger, more harmonious whole. It's easy to get fixated on the plan of the room and forget about volume. A handy way of thinking about volume is to visualize a room as positive and negative space: every piece of furniture you put in is positive, and all the air that is not occupied by furniture is negative. Don't disperse things too widely: control the positive in order to maintain enough negative space to let each piece register.

How do you keep a space from becoming too saturated? Even if a room is fifty-five feet long, don't bulk it up with furniture.

PAGES 80–81

Space-savers: a desk is tucked into a closet-sized alcove paneled in mahogany.

OPPOSITE

My clients already owned this handsome table and the beautifully carved Windsor chairs. I designed the spare chandelier; it manages to feel both modern and antique, and it reiterates the circle of the table.

ABOVE

A stalwart Mission table and chairs can stand up to a carpet with a strong geometric pattern. The Arts and Crafts cupboard looks like a small building; it repeats the furniture's straight lines but adds a few curves too.

Lighten it with more skeletal pieces. Keep a low horizon line to the
furniture, to liberate the space above. Composing a room is like
writing music—you need exciting passages, and then moments to
rest your eye. I find that if you overload a room with too much
surface decoration, then the patterns sponge up the negative space.
When I'm on the verge of going overboard, I sometimes discipline
myself by thinking about Shaker furniture, which has no
embellishment to confuse the eye.

Negative space brings out the individuality of the furniture,
but that doesn't mean it has to be expensive. I have things in my
house that are good, and things that are not so good. But they all
have character.

CIRCLES AND SQUARES

If you're lucky enough to have an octagonal room, why not go with the flow and complete the circle? A round pedestal table works well because the base is roughly circular. The two matching cabinets are ingeniously integrated into the architecture. The round carpet not only adds drama but also helps soundproof an unusually tall room.

In one of my first courses at the Rhode Island School of Design, I was asked to draw something without lifting my pencil from the paper. It was a good reminder that things should be continuous. A room is a volume. Your eye starts at one place and finishes at another. There should be a rhythm and a clarity of line. That's why I like circles. The line is never broken; it completes itself.

Curves are agents of change and mobility: the continuously curving line leads your eye to the next point. I find that without a circle—whether a round table, an oval portrait, or the round back rest on a chair—a room becomes a little stagnant. Squares are symbols of stability. I always use circular pieces in juxtaposition to squares, playing one off the other: they keep each other from getting boring, and together they animate a space.

In any room, gallery, or auction house, I inevitably gravitate to circles. Even the abstract paintings I pick often include circles. The circles don't have to be large to activate the space: circular lampshades, even bowls on a table, catch the eye. Round tables are dynamic— they spin the space. The circle works in elevation as well as plan: chairs with a circular backrest work the same magic in the vertical dimension, and a row of chairs with arched tops generates the same energy as the arches in a colonnade. I think of the lines like a rock skimming water, ducking and draking across the room. If you look at a Renaissance sketch of a cathedral facade, you can see how esoteric geometric studies of space can be. Playing with circles and squares

often gives you implied triangles that help you build a wall or a space. A circular mirror above a fireplace, for example, forms the top of a triangle whose base is the mantel. The invisible edges of the triangle hold the composition together. For these implied geometries to bind the parts together the pieces must be within visual reach of each other; otherwise, they're stranded. A carpet is very handy for defining the underlying shapes that hold an ensemble together. These visible and invisible geometries give a room discipline and a sense of stability and quiet.

CIRCULAR ROOMS Most circular rooms are for dining, and though I often put a circular table in a square room, I rarely try to fit a square table in a circular one: the corners create pinch points unless the room is large. I don't even put a square rug in a circular room.

A chandelier over the table will not only point out the center but also verticalize it—you want to center the room in three dimensions, not just two. In a house I did in California, the circular dining room had a vaulted ceiling from which we hung a Venetian glass chandelier that was a dramatic celebration of the room's center.

As always, don't forget the chairs: their ring is like a ripple out from the center. To reinforce the geometry, pick chairs with curved rather than straight lines. You might want high-backed chairs that make the table seem like a room within a room.

SCALE AND PROPORTION

Understanding scale—from the size of a room to the size of the furniture—is a helpful way to organize a room. Big and small spaces both have specific characteristics that play out in the furniture plan.

A big room, say, fifty feet long, is a gift of the real estate gods, and it's becoming more common with America's increasing infatuation with lofty spaces. But a big open space is not so easy to fill. I usually divide large spaces into smaller ones, creating rooms within the room. Carpets work especially well as space definers. Of course, they should be chosen with care to conform to the geometry of the room. If they're too narrow or too short, there's no harmony. The carpet should be placed to align with prominent architectural features. In one of the spaces I designed, three large windows supported the idea of dividing the room into three parts. But three is the limit to the number of area rugs even a large room can take—you just can't blanket a room with prayer rugs.

Scale brings up the issue of proportion, which Donald Judd once called "reason made visible." Discussions of proportion may seem arcane—they usually come with line drawings that illustrate divine mathematical ratios—but if you put twelve-year-olds in a room with pencil

and paper and ask them to draw a rectangle, they'll usually rediscover the Golden Mean all by themselves: we all feel the harmony.

PLAYING WITH SCALE From Renaissance Mannerists to Philippe Starck, plays of scale have been the province of masterly design comedians. Placing a huge piece of furniture next to a pipsqueak throws off the balance and stirs feelings of delight and surprise. Large-scale objects can fool the eye into thinking the rest of the room is on the same scale. You can exaggerate the height of the fireplace with a new mantel, or hang curtains from the ceiling to make a room feel taller, or bracket a seating group with unusually tall lamps. There are many things in a room that you can pull up in scale to give it more impact. But you still need the small to understand the large, and having a gradient of sizes in between bridges the two extremes. That's where the harmony comes in. You establish a visual relationship between two very different sizes through an object in a third size. Big scale jumps are arresting, but in smaller homes they can be too abrupt and hard to live with.

Tudor craftsmen had the right idea. The timber structure of this barn is so beautiful that it was an easy decision to keep it exposed. I love all the colors in the rustic stone floor. I added some fine Americana, like the prancing weathervane, the primitive portrait, and a jovial Uncle Sam.

FOUR CASE STUDIES

It's hard to talk about furniture plans in the abstract. The circles, squares, and plays of scale that make up balanced arrangements are difficult to grasp unless you can see them in context. So here are four case studies that illustrate various problems and explain the thought process I went through to come up with a furniture plan.

I. SAVING SPACE You do not need a wealth of pieces or a big room to create an elegant space. In the long, narrow living room of a client's one-bedroom apartment, I used only two sofas and a chair to create a seating area that is comfortable, commodious, and spare. Most people with a living room like this would place their sofa at the far end right under the window, but this strategy cuts off the window and wastes most of the space: the near end of the room becomes a doormat to the sofa. Even if you add two chairs opposite the sofa, that leaves a big hole at the other end of the apartment.

I discovered that by placing two long sofas opposite one another and parallel to the walls, I could take advantage of the full length of the room while framing the window as a focal point. It became clear that placed against the walls, the sofas would have too much space in between to work as a good conversational grouping. So I brought them away from the walls and tied them together with a substantial mahogany coffee table. Oddly enough, the simple gesture of pulling furniture away from the walls makes the apartment look much bigger. I left enough space between the sofas, the coffee table, and the walls so that you could easily walk to the window. I dimensioned the plan so that it would work when the room is full of people and still offer an intimate corner when the client is alone.

OPPOSITE
Pulling the sofas away from the wall creates the impression of more space in a long, narrow room.
BELOW
A small pedestal table is conveniently placed near the English Regency barrel chair.

The sofas, which are upholstered in a creamy camel chenille that sets off the dark frames, are positioned in a way that creates a room within the room because of their high-backed shape. The frames and boxlike volume of the sofas anchor a space that is otherwise recessive. The design of the furniture reinforces the idea in the plan: grouping as the main event. An English Regency barrel chair and deliberately mismatched side tables (matched tables would be too predictable) act as satellites around this fixed core.

The shell reads clearly as a volume. Simple white cabinets mask the obtrusive columns that were on either side of the window and provide more storage space. Now the window appears to be recessed between the cabinets, which could almost be read as structural piers supporting the ceiling beams, which were cleaned up and left exposed. At the near end, next to a closet and wet bar hidden behind paneled doors, a desk is built into an alcove paneled in mahogany. Tucking functional accessories into neat, out-of-the-way compartments leaves the overall space uncluttered.

LEFT
In this small living room, we kept it simple, using dark wood on the sofas, picture frames, and mirror.

OPPOSITE
Fresh flowers add vibrant color to the room.

2.

WORKING TOGETHER If you have two rooms right next to each other, you can create the impression that each is bigger by fostering the illusion that they are part of one large space. In this gracious apartment, the living room and dining room were natural partners. The furniture plan of each room has its own logic, but the rooms also work together as a suite. The secret is to create a certain ambiguity in the floor plan so that the spaces work both independently and as half of the whole.

I set up the living room in this glorious turn-of-the-century apartment by creating a double geometry so that one seating group

BELOW LEFT

A console table under the Venetian mirror in the dining room can also double as a sideboard for serving.

BELOW RIGHT

Texture play: a crystalline lamp against French silk taffeta curtains.

serves the living room and the other relates to the dining room and pulls the two together. The first group is anchored by a sofa, which sits with its back between the windows and is focused on the fireplace. Pairs of tables and chairs reinforce the formality of the room.

Just outside the seating area, which is defined by a carpet, and not more than a couple of feet beyond the carpet, I placed another sofa. The two side chairs on the carpet can pivot toward the second sofa, acting as spatial hinges connecting the main grouping to the outside sofa. This sofa has another life: it kicks off the second

The sofa on the left faces a fireplace and the other looks toward the adjacent dining room. It makes sense to have the major seating elements face a focal point in the room.

geometry by focusing on the dining room. I placed the sofa on an axis with the double doors leading to the dining room, where I set the dining table along the same line. Over the sofa I hung a large mirror to terminate one end of the living room; opposite it, in the dining room, the axis culminates in a painting. A nineteenth-century Russian chandelier, with fragile crystal pendants suspended from a gilt armature, hangs over the table, marking the center of the room.

Beyond geometry, the furniture reinforces the continuity. Oriental rugs of a similar scale and color in each room—a Sultanabad in the living room and a Tabriz in the dining room—form a visual pair, even if the doors divide them. All the furniture is French and, though of different periods, related. The pieces show a lot of leg, but at least these legs are attractive. In the dining room a filmy Venetian mirror dissolves any sense of rigidity in a fog of hand-painted tendrils and figures from the Commedia dell'Arte.

OPPOSITE
A fragment of an architectural frieze is the centerpiece of this mantelpiece vignette.

RIGHT
The Venetian mirror reflects a built-in china cupboard.

As varied as these accessories
are, they work in unison on
this tabletop.

OPPOSITE

Art and furniture need not
come from the same period.

3. ISLAND LIFE

Sometimes the interior of a home is just not the center of attention. In a quietly grand house overlooking the dunes on Long Island, the furnishings take a back seat to the view: the glory is outside.

The architects opened the spacious ground floor to the landscape with a long series of French doors. The suite of rooms here, from the library through the living room to the dining room, open on to each other with wide, double pocket doors. Inside, down the spine of the house, a long, ceremonial gallery runs the length of the three rooms. After the three large fireplaces are subtacted from the remaining walls, there is hardly any wall left. This is my kind of house.

The Swiss-cheese system of walls automatically made the decision for me—I would float islands of furniture into the space of

each room. There weren't even any corners to hide in. I established my design territory in the living room and the adjacent dining room with carpets that left a wide border exposing the hardwood floor. In the living room I used an uncompetitive rug with a light grid pattern.

In rooms with the openness of a pavilion, you have to ground the space with furniture. In the living room I created two groupings facing each other across the midline. Each grouping is anchored by a sofa. A pair of French wing chairs faces one sofa, while two upholstered chairs flank the other, along with an open-armed bergère. My clients had no interest in ostentation, and I didn't want the interior to upstage a pair of powerful but understated paintings by Susan Norrie. What gave the setting gravity was the sense of unity between the carpet and the upholstery on the voluminous chairs and sofas.

In the dining room my island was a French, midnineteenth-century round table that is large enough for big family gatherings. The diameter matches the nearby fireplace and seems to fit within its warm embrace. Its geometry fosters conversations, because nearly everyone faces everyone else.

LEFT
In a room where a lot of the wall space is taken up by French doors, you can still furnish against that wall if you pull the furniture forward.

OVERLEAF
The repetition of the big, bold shape of the Susan Norrie paintings pulls both sides of the room together and unifies the space.

In this dining room
composed of light walls
and dark woods, I like
the symmetry of the
circular chandelier above
the round table.

4. SAVING GRACE Some people are fortunate enough to have very large rooms, but furniture arrangements simply can't stretch infinitely to fill the void. If on top of that you have four doors leading to other rooms, you've got a traffic problem.

In a rambling shingle-style house in the Hamptons, the living room was generous at twenty-three feet by thirty feet and was crossed by three axes, including two for circulation. This confluence of large size and broken layout amounted to an SOS: it was up to the furniture plan to rescue the living room by breaking down the space into conversation-size groupings that could defend themselves from the highways cutting through. Two architectural features—a big fireplace and a bay window—also competed with one another for attention.

As in a military campaign, sometimes you conquer a room by dividing it. This time I organized the space into three furniture groupings. I staked out my territory with a rug stretching between the chimney and the wall opposite, being careful not to

RIGHT

This Hamptons shingle-style house was built by Robert A.M. Stern, Architects.

OVERLEAF

A pair of circular end tables throws a few more curves into this living room ensemble.

infringe on the flanking pathways, where people could trip. On the rug I created two furniture groupings: a sofa bracketed by two side tables and two club chairs that occupy the end next to the wall. Near the fireplace, two love seats face each other across a coffee table. I turned the carpet into a virtual four-poster by placing lights in each of the four corners. The furniture as an arrangement had to have a certain mass to stand up to some large, gutsy paintings.

That left the bay window, which forms an empty eddy off one of the passageways. I chanced on a curved 1920s bench in Paris and instantly knew, without even stopping to measure, that it would fit perfectly into the space. Two comfortable chairs and a coffee table turned the bay window into an inviting spot. A grand piano was planned for the passageway opposite.

If you are furnishing a hotel, you have to keep traffic lanes clear, but in a house, I like to walk through furniture. The passageways are still there, but so are the chairs.

BELOW

The room offers three distinct seating areas.

OPPOSITE

When you have a painting as bold as the Roy Lichtenstein above the fireplace, you need a strong furniture arrangement.

5. Putting It All Together

Designing a room involves a continuous give-and-take between the ideal and the real, a process of negotiation between what you imagine and what exists.

NOW THAT YOU HAVE A CONCEPT for the room and the start of a plan, the fun really begins. At last you can go shopping for the pieces you need to make it all come together. Slip on your walking shoes and take your ideas out for a test run. Check out the showrooms, flea markets, and auction houses to see what's available—and what you can afford. Designing a room involves a continuous give-and-take between the ideal and the real, a process of negotiation between what you imagine and what exists. Don't be discouraged if you don't find the coffee table of your dreams right away. Just because you're going to the stores doesn't necessarily mean you're going to lay out your credit cards. You may decide you can't do any better than what you already own. But one way or another, you'll come back from your rounds with a much better grasp of the possibilities. A shopping expedition also lets the element of surprise into the equation—you never know what you'll chance on, so keep your eyes and mind open.

Don't let your box of clippings from decorating magazines confuse you. Some clients come to me with a pile of photographs, but they don't understand that they can't have all those things in one room. People who aren't designers look at something eye-

In this drawing room, two low-slung chairs balance the wood-framed sofa, and the Italian armchair can move around to accommodate a conversation. The patterns on the upholstered chairs and the Spanish rug are practically equivalent in visual scale and weight, which creates a harmonious ensemble.

catching in a showroom and say, "Oh, that's pretty," but they don't think about what it would be like to live with that piece for a long time. Remember, when you pull out your checkbook you're committing your room to furniture that may be there for years. After your first spontaneous burst of enthusiasm for a piece, look it over very carefully and weigh its merits. Generally, it's a good idea to stick to things that work smoothly into your concept, and then you can build from there.

Price alone may affect your concept. Generally, simplicity is less expensive than a more formal setting. The size of a room can also help determine your approach: you can afford to be more elaborate in a smaller room. Large, traditionally furnished rooms gobble up furniture.

But where to begin?

CARPETS AND RUGS

Most designers use the terms carpet and rug interchangeably, so for nondesigners it can get tricky trying to decipher what we mean. For our purposes, I'll call everything a carpet unless I am specifically referring to an area rug. On the theory that the tail shouldn't wag the dog, I start with the bigger pieces, and that usually means the carpet. Think of it as the ground you're building on. If you choose a light-colored carpet, the furniture will seem to float. Darker colors, such as charcoal, navy, or green, anchor the room and the furniture. In most rooms, the carpet sets the palette and then you pick up the various colors in it through the upholstery. It makes sense to cross-reference colors to integrate the furniture and floor covering into an ensemble, because you don't want the floor to refuse the furniture. That would be a losing battle.

The style of the carpet could determine the style of the room, but you still can't choose it without thinking of the concept of a room. The carpet and the room have to convey the same feelings. You could think of it as sharing the same mood. A wool Tabriz, which is a Persian rug with richly colored reds and blues in geometric patterns, reinforces a stately living room, while a simple cotton dhurrie, woven in solid colors or stripes, suits a casual house. If you've always longed for a gloriously figured Aubusson but aren't prepared to take out a second mortgage to pay for it, consider this: your rug doesn't have to be an antique. New versions are being made that are more affordable. In a library or bedroom, try an Axminster, which is a very fine, tight-loop English weave that seems to suit smaller spaces.

When I'm choosing among several different carpets, all other things being equal, I look for depth of color. If it's too strongly colored and flat, the carpet is visually not going to sit on the floor and will always intrude (unless you turn up the chromatic volume on the whole room to compensate). The scale and intricacy of the pattern also have to work in the context of the space. In a pared-down room, an intricately patterned rug requires that everything else get a lot quieter.

Given the option, I always prefer old: a softly shaded, venerable carpet just has more soul. There are certain new carpets that have the character and variegation of antiques. Those from Tibet have a lovely, mellow look with a very thick, luxurious pile and subtle, rich shadings. Those with just a plain field of pale color are my personal favorites. Often the carpetmaker couldn't resist weaving in little embellishments throughout the carpet—such as tiny triangles the size of a dime—that, I'm told, are messages to God.

— Border Policy —

◆   If the rug you choose has a border, you have to consider the size and shape of the border relative to the size and shape of the room. If they don't match up, it throws off the eye.

◆   To be safe, stay away from wide borders and center medallions because they limit your maneuverability. When you're arranging furniture, the rule of thumb is to furnish within the border. But don't worry if the most logical arrangement has some of the legs crossing the edge to stand on the floor. The room will survive.

SOFAS

The upholstery on the sofa and chairs will probably be the next big stroke of color in the room, after the carpet, so of course they have to agree. If you have a really strong rug, you should pull back on the upholstery. The colors of a new carpet may mellow with time, but you can't fight a bold pattern. You have to compensate or adjust elsewhere to achieve the sense of balance that is so important if you want to create an inviting room. Patterned upholstery can be tricky against a patterned carpet, so you may want to retreat to a self-effacing, small-scale pattern or play it safe with a quiet beige, cream, camel, or khaki. Some people avoid white-on-white, but I think it is very elegant. If the upholstery has little color, it should have some interesting texture, like raw silk, pure cotton, natural linen, silk velvet, or chenille. I put the strongest color or pattern on the floor and pick it up later in a piece of art, a lamp, or a pillow—but not in anything as large as a sofa. A skirt, whether shirred or pleated, makes a sofa more formal; it's more modern when you can see the legs.

How much sofa will a room tolerate? If you spot something you like, make sure you go home with the measurements from a salesperson so that you can make sure it's the appropriate size for your room. Standard overall measurements for the length of a sofa are sixty, seventy-two, eighty-four,

I love to take fragments of antique fabrics and turn them into throw pillows.

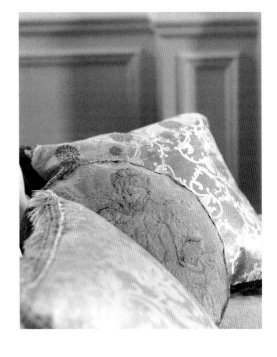

or ninety-six inches, but there is no magic formula to tell you what size you should choose for your room. Pull out the plan you made earlier, do a scale drawing of the sofa you like, and see how it fits in the room. Ask yourself whether it would look better if it were bigger or smaller. Some people like a sofa that's big and perfect for afternoon naps. Others prefer a cozy loveseat that doesn't take up too much space. The desired depth of the seat cushions depends on the size of the individual who's going to use it. The standard overall depth is thirty-six inches, but you'll want to go deeper if there's a tall person in the sofa's future. Before you go all out, remember: the average person doesn't feel comfortable sitting on something six inches deeper than the standard. A deeper sofa works only in a family room, where you can put your feet up and watch a movie.

Keep the cushions simple. If you want a sofa you can sleep on, one long cushion is more accommodating than a trio or a pair, but it's easier to sit on smaller cushions that won't rise up around you in a V.

I like to use down in my cushions, because it's so pliant and luxurious, but instead of using 100 percent down, I put in a thin piece of foam rubber at the core to stabilize the form. Otherwise, you sink in when you sit on it for a while, and when you get up, there's a depression. I never use artificial materials such as Dacron to stuff a cushion if I can help it. It's "poly-something" and "poly" means plastic, which just doesn't have the right feel.

CHAIRS

When in doubt, think chairs. I'm a chair addict. I'm not above using them for purposes other than seating; sometimes I stack them with books. One or two interesting chairs go a long way toward building the personality of a room. They don't have to be a matched pair, but it helps if you mate chairs of the same genre—like two Edwardian hall chairs left over from the time when there were still footmen. Character chairs like these shouldn't be saved for formal rooms, because they work all through the house.

OPPOSITE

A love seat just fits on the wall by the door.

ABOVE

In an alcove of this Long Island home, we paired an American wicker chair and a marquetry cabinet from the same period.

LEFT

This is a favorite dining chair of mine. Because the whole piece is upholstered, including the arms, you can sit comfortably at the table for hours without squirming.

When choosing a desk chair, make sure it has the right scale so that the legs fit into the kneehole of the desk.

ABOVE RIGHT

Every room needs at least one character chair. Here, a child's chair is drawn up to the hearth.

Unfortunately, you can't just walk into a furniture store and ask for a character chair—you've got to sleuth them out in unexpected places. Hit the brakes when you pass an intriguing antique store, or follow up on an estate-sale ad in a local paper. I always enjoy the time spent looking.

When I see a promising chair, I do apply some standards before buying it. Chairs should look as good from the back as from the front. If you're going to feature them in a room, perhaps placing them at an angle to the sofa, you'll probably be seeing them in the round, so all sides count. Look for an interesting silhouette. Bentwood chairs, with

their thin strips of wood molded into a curve, are like calligraphy in space. A well-rubbed arm invites the touch, and natural wood lends a sense of authenticity and gravitas to a room.

Of course, it's nice if an occasional chair is comfortable, but frankly I'd rather sit on a sofa and look at the chairs. They're like people to me. I think of them as company (although I don't talk to them, yet). In my office I keep a pair of eighteenth-century Belgian Empire chairs, which I bought in a store on Route 7 in Connecticut in 1966. They have gracefully scrolled arms. I'm very attached to them. They're old friends.

A cluster of cushions creates the
ultimate reading nook at a window
overlooking the water.

UPHOLSTERY

An exceptional chair is an opportunity for exceptional upholstery, but of course, it should relate to other colors and patterns in the room. You can be more daring and experimental here by using an old tapestry weave, needlepoint, cowhide, or suede, which you wouldn't use to cover big surfaces or a matching suite of furniture.

If opting for a solid color, consider quilting the fabric and adding tufting or nailheads, depending, of course, on the style of the chair. The chair and its upholstery should have a little conversation that's lively, not literal. I don't necessarily use period upholstery on an antique.

Reupholstering an antique chair can reduce its value, and if your intent is to be archivally correct, you should leave it alone. But unless you want to live in a museum, reupholstering is almost a given.

Old fabric is often moth-eaten and mildewed. A good upholsterer can steer you to an appropriate replacement, and your chair will emerge refreshed.

If you need to find a good upholsterer, collect recommendations from friends and take a close look at each upholsterer's work. When you visit the workroom, be very specific about what your expectations are, and be sure that the upholsterer intends to take off the old fabric before putting on the new. That way, you'll get a firmer seat. A good upholsterer can become your partner in design, suggesting embellishments such as a contrasting gimp or trim. Certain styles suit certain rooms.

A more formal room might get a chair with more elaborate upholstery, such as an elegant

I found a pair of nineteenth-century Continental pier mirrors that had the right scale for the room and were a good accompaniment to the delicate console tables.

slipper chair with tiny buttons down the back. I stop before the fabric becomes so conspicuous that it's no longer integrated into the room. For slipcovers, I recommend simple white muslin. It's always fresh, light, and appealing and can turn the dowdiest relic into Cinderella for the summer.

In choosing fabric, follow your heart. When you find something you truly love, buy it—even if it means spending a little more money. I think of fabric as an investment, because you'll keep something you like for a very long time.

Inverted pleats add a little kick to this sofa.

6. THE DELICATE BALANCE

*The delicate balance may be serene
but it should not be boring.*

THERE IS A STRONG classicizing impulse in my rooms: the chairs, tables, and sofas may be from different countries and disparate periods, but I balance the elements by arranging them in symmetrically ordered hierarchies. The harmony comes from a sense of agreement among the parts, the relationship of one thing to another within groupings that I balance around a center. The parts add up to a whole.

PREVIOUS PAGES

Hammered silver vases, Venetian mask molds, and silver candlesticks are paired on the mantelpiece, next to an Italian artist's mannequin.

LEFT

I paired two line drawings over a neoclassical-style cabinet to create an ensemble strong enough to anchor a living room corner. The combination of dark cabinet and light pictures sets up a lovely balance of black and white.

BALANCING THE FLOOR AND THE WALL

The floor and wall are part of the same continuum of surfaces that wraps the space, and they should work in a dynamic equilibrium. Often the wall is the weak link. Once, in a project that had ample windows in a wide, rectangular room, I installed substantial window seats to give the walls volume. I did it on both sides of the room to give it balance. Otherwise, the room would have tipped to one side.

Balance goes to the heart of everything I do, and I weigh the walls against the floor in terms of color, style, and the size and scale of the elements on each in order to achieve that balance. Many people, especially those who haven't developed a personal art collection, have to make a special effort to love their walls. Think of the wall as the equivalent of a carpeted floor. How would you want to build it up? Both horizontal and vertical surfaces should have a complementary weight and complexity. A great painting demands its own space. If you don't have strong wall pieces, such as a distinctive mirror or a few good paintings, you can compensate by organizing charming smaller prints into compositions. They might achieve their strength in a geometric cluster over a console set off by silver accessories. If you are lucky enough to have powerful paintings or wall hangings, then the right balance calls for clearing a lot of floor space to shift the focus to the wall; you have no need for an ornate carpet.

This composition is all about triangles, starting with that tiny triangle in the center of the Howard Buchwald painting, which prompted me to choose three vases and three colors—white, blue-green, and red.

EQUILIBRIUM The tried and true way of establishing equilibrium is to start by building out from the fireplace, but not all rooms have that mythic hearth. Everybody loves flowers, and they can be chosen for the shape they create. I've balanced a bookcase on one wall with a tall, generous bouquet atop a console on the matching wall, to keep that whole side of the room from just falling away. A pair of club chairs or love seats or the right sofa can anchor a room as a fireplace does, by creating a pole around which the room is organized. Or start at the perimeter and occupy the four corners of the room with pieces of equal weight. Or bisect a room with a table and balance the two halves with different groupings of equal interest.

The building block of my room is not the individual piece but the pair. If you choose carefully, each thing is interesting, and what you see once, you want to see again. If everything is single and alone, there's less continuity. An isolated table or chair only amounts to a point in space, but a group of two creates a small geometry that can tie into the room's larger geometry.

You can put two or more strong patterns in the same room as long as they have equivalent weights. The pattern on the chair seats is just as robust as the pattern in the carpet. In a way, they cancel each other out.

TOP

I decided that the black lampshades on the slender silver desk lamps would be just the thing to set off the vaporous whites of the Agnes Martin painting.

ABOVE

A strong concept was needed to make something of the walls flanking a front doorway. I settled on four pairs: two alabaster sconces, two oval mirrors, two silver candlesticks, and two bracketed shelves.

RIGHT

Instead of dedicating this dining room to just one function, I decided it could do double-duty as a library. The table is big enough to spread out papers and use as a desk.

In any room, you need more than one lamp, so necessity encourages you to think in pairs, in order to establish a rhythm and to create symmetry. The layout of most rooms would probably preclude putting lamps in all four corners, but you could reinforce the geometry of the room by placing lamps in two corners. They should be in near rather than distant corners; otherwise, the eye won't make the connection. The lampshades and height of both lamps should stay the same, to keep the space settled and calm. Just because you have paired lamps doesn't mean you can't bring in a different desk lamp, or another odd-lamp-out, as necessary.

Old-fashioned glass-front cabinets create their own geometry in the kitchen.

— *Using Pairs* —

I couple almost any kind of furniture or accessory—
tables, mirrors, paintings, lamps—and then I balance the pairs.

◆ Sofas work well as pairs facing each other in the middle of a room, at a window, or in front of a fireplace. Mantels cry out for pairs of vases, candlesticks, or pictures.

◆ When a room doesn't come with good architectural features, use a pair of boldly shaped chairs to lend it structure. They bracket space and create a sense of place within the room.

◆ A door can be the occasion for a pair of mirrors, consoles, chairs, or sconces placed along the wall on either side.

◆ Mirrors can be the mates of windows, and I often hang them on the wall opposite or adjacent to the windows, creating virtual pairs.

◆ A set of paired drawings has more presence than either drawing would have alone. Hung over a side table or console and stacked one over the other, the drawings have even more impact than they would if hung side by side.

This house is done in the
classic American Federal
style, which is all about
pairs and balances. When
you walk through the center
hall, you turn right into the
living room (pictured) or
left into the dining room.
Only two pairs of Ionic
columns separate the huge
space. Window treatments
and hanging lanterns are
identical to unify the two
rooms. Two similarly
colored carpets define each
seating arrangement.

MIX IT UP The delicate balance may be serene but it should
not be boring. I break up the pairing before any monotony sets
in, and boredom usually arrives with the third pair. For a measure
of surprise, mix modern pieces with antiques so that the room is
neither completely traditional nor contemporary. (The ambiguity
lends timelessness.) I might toss an austere Jacobean chair, made
out of dark, highly carved wood, into a symmetrical arrangement
of sleek, white contemporary sofas. Qualities like mass, color,
texture, and size are all variable elements of the mix. My style is
neither modern nor traditional, but I do look at classical pieces
with a modernist eye. I study the form and structure of a piece
and imagine how it'll look with enough space around it so it can
breathe, rather than locked into a crowded arrangement.

You should develop a sense of when to break the symmetry
you've carefully constructed. My
personal panacea is to simply pull
up an eccentric chair when a conversational grouping gets too pat. I let
the piece just float in at an angle.
Of course, this kind of exceptional
piece has to be interesting to deserve
the attention it will get and to justify
itself as the interloper. A writing
table at a window could just as well
be the exceptional piece that breaks
the rhythm.

Consistency, Emerson said,
is the hobgoblin of little minds. So
instead of hanging a chandelier in
every room or using sconces

throughout, I sometimes center the dining room with a crystal piece over the main table and use a more modern approach, such as recessed halogen spotlights, in the hall. I can get traditional again in the library by using a brass fixture in the ceiling along with a pair of wall sconces.

RIGHT

The bookcases become an architectural element, a study in symmetry.

OPPOSITE

Adjacent to the living room is the mahogany-paneled library, with a classical glass transom over the door.

— Mixing Well —

Things to remember when mixing styles:

◆ The scale has to agree: don't swamp a fragile antique side chair with a voluminous sofa. Instead, use a loveseat, which is more in sync with the proportions. And don't forget to consider the scale of the architecture. You need large-scale elements in a high-ceilinged room.

◆ Shift scales for a more dramatic effect when using pairs. Mirrors or paintings can be slightly smaller or taller than one another.

◆ You don't always need identical twins to create a sense of balance. Play opposites against each other— straight and curved, shiny and matte, patterned and plain, vertical and horizontal, or square and circle. An organically shaped Chinese root table is the perfect podium for a finely wrought silver candlestick and a geometrically shaped glass lamp.

◆ Spend the surprise in a room on pieces that are interesting and exceptional.

◆ A triangular arrangement of objects may draw attention to a focal point, but balancing two against one works only if the pair and the singular object have equivalent weights. Two substantial chairs can stand up to an imposing sofa.

◆ Within a clearly ordered scheme, asymmetry registers with much more impact. If you have a very interesting, singular piece, feature it by placing it outside the symmetry. Break the order with the exception.

◆ Establish a common level to keep the room calm. I usually keep paired lamps and other background pieces at matching heights.

The rough, organic shape of the Chinese root table sets off the man-made— a silver candlestick and a glass lamp. I had individual glass beads hand-sewn along the bottom of the lampshade to catch the light. Sometimes beauty is worth the extra effort.

WATCHING YOUR WEIGHT

The issue of weight is crucial to balance. A slim console table is probably inadequate to counterbalance a large ornate mirror. I weigh masses visually and allow gravity to pull heavier pieces near the floor; letting heavy things settle creates a sense of repose and inevitability. I like to leave the upper reaches vacant and airy, the ethereal whites drifting away.

ABOVE

And now for something
completely different—
Chinese embroidered
sweaters from the
1940s are reincarnated
as pillow covers.

OPPOSITE

A trim such as a traditional
cord or a fanciful ball fringe
adds panache to any pillow.

BALANCING PATTERNS I generally stay away from
patterned fabrics, though I may use one in small quantities on
limited surfaces when it's not going to be pronounced. If there's
no strong architecture in the shell, then using a pattern makes a
lot of sense, because you can build a room from it.

In the small or very plain room, you can achieve an automatic
balance by covering everything in the same fabric, even the walls.
Fabric can be inexpensive, so you can use a lot of it. The space
automatically becomes a seamless field. Your eye doesn't go to
one object, because one piece blends into another and you see the

whole. An all-over pattern expands space
because the edges and boundaries dissolve,
erasing a room's limits. In a tiny bedroom of
mine in London, I used stripes on the walls,
ceiling, draperies, and headboard and went
with a complementary pattern on the canopy—
another fabric in the same exact tone. The
effect was harmonious, and more intriguing
than a perfect match.

If you would like a touch of pattern, it can
help you reinforce the balance in a room. You
might use a very exaggerated pattern, like a
cabbage rose, everywhere in a bedroom, or on
opposite sides of a living room, or surrounding
just one library doorway: your eye fills in the
blanks. With a smaller-scale pattern, whether
a check, stripe, or miniature motif, you can
balance a room by using the fabric in several
places, such as on the cushions and a footstool.
It takes two or three small-patterned pieces to

stand up to one big-patterned piece. If you mix checks and stripes in one room, make sure each pattern shares the same weight and tone. Often a tiny print will make a small room feel even smaller, so use it when you want that kind of intimacy.

Pattern carries a lot of power and can work like a secret weapon to balance or unify a room. Just one note of caution: if you're falling in love with a particular fabric, try to visualize it in the size you need. It always helps to have a really big sample, which makes it easier to understand how the finished piece will look.

OPPOSITE
A classically proportioned room feels relaxed and contemporary, with furniture pared down to a few well-chosen pieces and objects selected for their sculptural strength, no matter what the era.

LEFT
Typically you would find bucolic landscapes on either side of the mirror, but I wanted something more startling and chose two overscale, out-of-focus photographs silk-screened on Lucite by Seton Smith. On the center table, a Mayan terra-cotta bowl provides a spiky counterpoint to a group of smooth African shackles, originally worn as a sign of wealth.

I try to use a balance of small, medium, and large patterns in every room. The ticking stripe on the chairs qualifies as small. Tattersall silk curtains provide the medium, and the 1920s Wiener Werkstatte—style carpet supplies the large. A simple conical chandelier hangs from the center of the ceiling and takes the stuffiness out of what could have been a very formal room.

7. Working with a Pale Palette

Color is one of life's great mysteries, and I'm endlessly fascinated and surprised by how it changes a room.

MANY PEOPLE ASSUME that there's no color in a room if you haven't plastered chintz over everything. That's not true. My rooms, which everyone thinks are creamy and white, are filled with color, but the colors don't scream.

I work in subtle shades of color and variations of patterns rather than in big blocks of solids and prints. I wouldn't normally go for high contrasts or conspicuous matching. For example, I wouldn't carry the yellow in a sofa over to the curtains while matching the pattern of the pillows to a side chair. That kind of obvious connect-the-dots approach kills a room. Don't get me wrong about yellow, red, or blue—I love them. They can play a role in any color scheme, but should do so in a quiet way.

There is no such thing as a bad color if it's used well. Color is a tool. I use it to order a room and to steer the eye. I prefer a neutral shell enhanced with satellites of color on the pillows or other accessories, which are easier to change.

Color is one of life's great mysteries, and I'm endlessly fascinated and surprised by how it changes a room.

A Word on
Using Color

Color should reinforce the architecture of a room. If you put all sorts of different colors in a space, you're dismantling the structure, breaking it into parts. Color is not a stand-alone statement but a basic way of bringing parts together. It's the cornerstone of what I call my grand unification strategy. If the colors of a room are not balanced in value and hue, then it's chaos. You can't put red here, blue there, orange someplace else, and hope for the best. You need to construct a frame of reference. If you put two equally saturated colors—for example, blue and green in the same intensity—in separate parts of the room, you achieve a balance. Two lamps with dark blue shades and a soft dark green sofa will create a triangle in an otherwise pale field. Sometimes colors reinforce other visual dynamics in a room. I've concentrated darker colors below a chair rail to lend visual weight to the

OPPOSITE

A palette of ivory, cream, and beige creates a restful atmosphere in this guest room.

ABOVE

I'm a big proponent of all-white beds. The Carolyn Brady painting on the mantel adds some color.

LEFT

Simple sheer curtains allow generous amounts of natural light into this master bath.

natural gravitational pull of the room. I use colors so discreetly that some of my rooms appear not to have any color in them at all, but they do. There is a big difference between white, ivory, and coffee. If you blend them the right way, they appear to be the same even though they are not.

The color of the walls dictates the impression of a room. I first lay claim to a room by disciplining the shell with paint. I keep surfaces continuous by turning the corners with the same color, extending it to the ceiling and often even to the floor. This kind of color keeps the eye moving, because you don't want it to stop at every corner. You want to see the room as a whole.

When I carry a color off the walls and onto the furniture, I'm using it to build a room. It's a form of repetition, and a way of making a color spatial—suddenly it's no longer flat. When you do this, you're taking two-dimensional walls into the third dimension by working in the round—it's almost like fashioning a piece of sculpture.

LEFT

In an all-white powder room, I added a little something old, with the sconces and mirror, and something bold, a zebra print mini-ottoman.

OPPOSITE

A mirrored 1930s-style night table almost levitates in this ivory bedroom.

Luxurious textures in several
shades of taupe add warmth
to this living room. Subtle
patterns on the upholstery
echo the muted rug.

BOLD COLOR

It can be exciting to let spirited colors take over in the powder room, the kitchen, or the library. In one commission I looked at paintings by Milton Avery, who has been a silent partner in many of my color schemes, and found shades ranging from a deep blue-green to a pale mauve. In another house, someone called me an herbalist for using colors such as verbena, sage, olive, mushroom, hemp, and vanilla.

I often use paints from a line by the color consultant Donald Kaufman because his colors are complex. His shades are composed of many different pigments, and as the light shifts different tones come out. That kind of richness and depth make a room feel more alive.

Old houses represent a special case. You almost need to put your ear to the wall to listen for the color history. The eighteenth century was all about colors, and sometimes they were shockingly loud and daringly bright. They sizzled—maybe because our ancestors were compensating for the dimness of candlelight. Strong color on the walls has consequences for the furniture. A room with deep colors doesn't silhouette the furniture, as happens in an all-white room. Deep colors mix the pieces like a stew, and you have to fill the room with even more color and furniture.

Antique-green silk damask
covers the walls in this
bedroom and creates a
vibrant backdrop for the
mahogany furniture and
the pale upholstery.

In a manor house in
Ireland, where it's often
gray outside, color inside
lifts the spirits.

The entrance hall is painted
sunny yellow with white
trim and ceiling.

— Color Sense —

◆ When you take a color from the walls to the curtains or carpets, vary it slightly to form a subtle tapestry woven through space. The weave might result from the mix of colors on the carpeting, the upholstery, ceramics—there are many materials with which you can "paint" a room. A big iron coffee table in a white room becomes a color, but it gets richer if you multiply it somewhere in the rug, on a table-top accessory, or with the base of a lamp.

◆ To maintain serenity, avoid high contrasts. Establish a rich variation within a narrow tonal range. Shifts in hue matter almost as much as fabrics and pieces of furniture. Choose objects that are not stark and isolated but have a family resemblance and work as an ensemble.

◆ It's the blend of colors that creates an atmospheric effect. My rooms hardly come out of the same bucket of paint. The simplicity is only apparent; the color scheme is actually complex.

RIGHT

The red carpet and green walls in the drawing room provide a rich backdrop for the collection of nineteenth-century landscapes.

OPPOSITE

Pale yellow glazed walls and a gray-toned carpet create a neutral backdrop for various shades of blue in a spacious London drawing room.

Deep red walls make a large
dining room feel more
intimate. The Waterford
crystal and Waterford
chandelier reflect the light.

WARMER SHADES OF PALE

People today lead active lives. They're out in a world that blasts them with color, from billboards to supermarket shelves. I think of the house as a sanctuary, and too much color there can be aggressive. You should be able to come home to a soothing environment, and I've found that a pale, off-white palette has a calming effect. Another benefit of using light colors is that they often make spaces look larger and ceilings higher; a subdued palette dematerializes walls and expands space. Also, in a less colorful space you can get away with fewer pieces of furniture. Neutral rooms let you use large-scale objects more easily. It frees the space.

At any paint store you'll find a hundred different shades of white—cream, vanilla, ivory, eggshell, alabaster. My whites are far from pure. I soften them so that they are not edgy and harsh. Adding a touch of yellow or cream has an effect like opening the windows: it airs out the room and lets in the sun.

LEFT
The play of light tones against dark walls brings out the fine bones of the mahogany paneling.

OPPOSITE
Neutral isn't necessarily white. In a mahogany-paneled library, shades of beige, brown, and coffee smoothly blend into a whole. The effect is tailored and handsome.

BRINGING OUT
THE ARCHITECTURE

White can help bring out the architectural features of a
room. In a traditional room, pick out the trim—moldings,
baseboard, window and door surrounds—in a white that's
whiter than the walls. If you really want to get subtle, change the
trim finish to a satin or high gloss to contrast with the surrounding
paint. When I renovated my barn, I painted the beams the same
white as the walls to give them equal weight. I once worked for
Edward Durrell Stone, one of the architects of the Museum of
Modern Art. His office, in a very elegant town house, was painted
white to defer to the architecture and the art. I remember he had a
Larry Rivers painting that looked so beautiful set against the white.

You should alter colors to suit the climate and region in which
you live. When working on a home in the desert, I add extra pigment
to a color to keep the intense sun from bleaching it. At the seashore,
I warm the whites with a sprinkle of yellow or red so that they don't
take on the overcast gray that you get on cloudy or hazy days.

The English and Irish have long apologized for the dreary
weather outside by using color inside their homes. British country
houses are full of yellows, reds, and bright blues to cheer these
places up.

Color has an immense effect on the human psyche. If you
deploy it judiciously, color can transform your mood and your house.

The living room of a new
California house, conceived
as a villa in a garden, recalls
Renaissance loggias. Two
pristine columns bring the
symmetries of the formal
landscape inside, where
a sofa with matching
love seats is centered on
the view. The creamy white
and pale yellow palette
reflects the sunlight and
heightens the open-air
feeling of the room.

8. THE ART OF LIVING WITH ART

Art follows furniture, not furniture art.

PREVIOUS PAGES

A client's childhood drawings were framed and placed in a row on the ledge of a master bathroom, making an architectural cornice out of personal history.

RIGHT

There's a wonderful rhythm between the Jean Dubuffet painting on the wall and the Sultanabad carpet on the floor. They should fight each other but they don't.

OPPOSITE

When you have paintings by Pablo Picasso and Paul Klee, and a sculpture by Henry Moore, you really can't go wrong.

LIFE IS FULL OF little detours, and I like to make as many as possible into Doyle's, the auction house up the block from my office. I often duck in just to refresh my eye. You never know what you're going to need all of a sudden. I usually manage to find some good things, and when I have the time to sort through them all, I always find that it was worth the stop. One afternoon, after a presentation to my clients, I decided to leave early and treat myself to a visit. When I stepped into the cluttered premium room, a pair of bell-jar lanterns hanging from the ceiling caught my eye. I sat down on a nearby sofa to get a better view of them and practically crushed an envelope that was lying there. It contained sixteen little pencil studies—very tender, almost hesitant sketches. I knew they were very good: when you're interested in art and expose yourself to a lot of material, you can tell. At the time I didn't have a place for them in mind, but at $2,000, I thought they were a good value. I bought the drawings and never looked back at the lanterns.

WHAT TO LOOK FOR

Once you've picked the colors for a room, done the layout, and chosen and placed the furniture, the great question mark is the empty wall: you need something to fill the blankness between the ceiling and the floor. Don't just resort to mirrors as the design panacea for the space over a sofa. The issue of paintings is often fudged because people confuse art with decor. The two aren't the same. The quality, color, framing, and location of a painting or print helps set the tone or character of a room, but you're shortchanging the art's potential as a free and wonderful agent if you treat it as an extension of the color scheme. Because of its focal position and privileged status, art plays a powerful role. It has the ability to embody the soul of a room: it's where the joy starts. Art is an accessory that's necessary.

My little detours into galleries, museums, and auction houses are both a pleasure and an exercise. Though I'm

PAGES 184–185
In a collector's New York
City apartment, the art
takes center stage. A modern
painting is the focal point
of the sitting room.

LEFT
A vibrant painting can
animate a dining room even
when it's empty of people.

When you have strong art
on the walls, you can be
bold with your color palette.
Don't think you have to
match the colors in the
upholstery to the colors
in the painting. That's the
quickest way to make a room
look like a greeting card.

only browsing, I'm developing background and a thousand points of comparison. Initially my interest was stirred when I studied art history in school, and doing houses for people who have wonderful art collections has deepened my sensitivity. When I am handling the work, I cultivate an appreciation for it because I have to understand the thinking of an artist to know how to best place his or her work. I've learned to spot quality and appreciate the

specifics, such as color and its impact on a space.

After everything else is said, painted, upholstered, and done, art can make the difference. You might save up for a really stellar piece and hang it alone in the living room—the glory of the space—or use several quiet, unassuming pieces to tie a room together. An automatic cohesion occurs when several works of art start melding into a collection. Of course, art needn't stop at the walls. It's very interesting to live with sculpture and to design layouts around it. You can also find pieces, like African masks, to put on tabletops. Even furniture can be considered art.

All my detours, big and small, have helped me develop a mini-expertise in art, and I've developed a method for zeroing in on what I want in a piece of art. For example, I have come to love portraits. Given their age, their prices are remarkably accessible. These paintings are not in great demand, because they have usually passed out of the family, and out of memory, landing in attics. I like to study the social and personal attitudes that the sitters express. I look at the clothes to understand the times. Curiously, it's harder to find a portrait of a pretty woman than a stately gentleman. Sometimes I introduce a single portrait of a man to an unaccompanied portrait of a woman and marry them off by hanging them together. Because they're usually formal, portraits help give a room structure.

OPPOSITE

You don't have to own a huge loft to hang a large painting, and don't fret if furniture stands in front of it. Something interesting happens when a canvas becomes atmospheric.

ABOVE

Modern art mingles with traditional furnishings.

PICK A GENRE

When you're choosing art for a room, it helps to have a concept. I often go against the grain by using contemporary art with traditional furniture, or some incredible period painting in a midcentury modern room full of Mies van der Rohe pieces. Somehow each element is enlivened by the other. But you have to be selective in the process. If you're doing this kind of contrast, limit the categories to two, playing one against the other. Otherwise, if there are too many shifts in a room, your eye doesn't understand the differences and you slip into the eclectic, which is another approach altogether.

If you want a room to feel coherent, you have to cultivate your preferences in art. If it's modern, go for that. If your taste is minimalist—like my preference for paintings with circles and squares—find and follow the artists with an affinity for geometry. There is so much out there from which to choose. Nineteenth-century paintings, often depicting people in houses, give you windows into other rooms and lives. Or you might like atmospheric landscapes, or exclusively American vistas, or European artists from a certain country. Once you find something you like, developing an expertise broadens your sphere of knowledge and trains your eye to be discerning.

In my own office, you can see my love for geometric shapes in the Jack Tworkov painting and the Calder-esque mobile.

MAKING ART AFFORDABLE

Of course, your range of art choices is determined by the depth of
your pockets: even the wealthiest art patrons have budgets and
can't afford that many Impressionists—it's very easy to run through
a fortune at Sotheby's. If you can write a check in the $10,000 to
$45,000 range, you can put a bold, contemporary painting on your
wall. Less than that might get you a substantial work by a little-
known but promising artist. If your budget is smaller, consider
works on paper. Lithographs are run off in limited editions, and
you can even get prints by some very established artists like Roy

Lichtenstein, Robert Indiana, and Robert Rauschenberg at prices that are less than frightening. Some people collect genres, like botanical prints and equestrian scenes. If you find an old book and take it apart (though the very thought makes bibliophiles cringe), you have an instant collection. Personally, I love watercolors—the transparency of the medium gives them a great delicacy—and they're usually less expensive than oil paintings.

Art schools are another place to look for affordable art. The drawings you see there are sometimes worth framing and hanging, if you have a self-confident eye. Flea markets can be a treasure trove of art. I found some wonderful architectural prints in the Paris flea market for a reasonable number of francs. Even Sotheby's and Christie's can be accessibly priced if you're clever—I remember watching a woman shuffle through several drawings on the floor in Christie's back room, but she overlooked a Richard Serra lithograph ($3,000), which certainly interested me and now hangs in my office. I bought some of the pieces I love best in SoHo and Chelsea galleries, but I've also acquired terrific art donated by parents at silent auctions at my children's schools.

OPPOSITE
Even the most humble objects can be beautiful. With the patina of age, these turn-of-the-century high-topped shoes have a strong collective presence when lined up by size and featured on an apothecary cabinet.

ABOVE
It's interesting to see all the possible variations on one simple form—whether a lusterware pitcher or a watering can.

COLLECTING AND DISPLAY

BELOW LEFT
Shelves instantly organize any
collection. The wooden boxes
look more intriguing when you
can compare and contrast.

BELOW RIGHT
A collection of blue-and-white
porcelain turns into art when it's
arrayed all together on a plate
rack in a kitchen.

OPPOSITE
A Regency console table with cast-
iron vases creates a virtual pedestal
for an arrangement of architectural
molds that I found in England.

Of course, a Picasso is a Picasso is a Picasso, and you don't
need to have more than one to change your life and your
living room. But even if you're fresh out of masterpieces,
you can still create a beautiful room by doing more with the
materials you already have on hand. Collecting is an impulse
deeply embedded in the human psyche, and the secret of
making your treasures look interesting is all in the art of
display. Instead of scattering objects around a room, group
them together for more impact: the whole is greater than the
sum of the parts. I once hung a room with one hundred blue-

and-white porcelain plates, and the collection became art. Even the most ordinary objects—teapots, tortoiseshell boxes, antique hatpins, watering cans—become interesting in quantity. I found a trove of fifteen vintage teapots, each slightly different, at a flea market and bought them for $1.50 each. They're going to sit on a shelf in my new kitchen, where my guests and I can admire them. You don't have to spend a fortune to make a statement that says something about you. A collection of tape measures on a table is far more unexpected than a Matisse over the fireplace, and it's more personal. Framed and grouped childhood drawings can be surprisingly powerful and spirited.

A collection of antique and modern crystal candlesticks captures the light and adds an individual touch to this tabletop.

A collection needn't occupy every surface or a primary location. It's much more intriguing if you see a whole collection of things displayed in some interesting fashion on the walls of a hall. Botanical prints can lure your eye into the nether corners. Things like shells, souvenir buildings, and art glass could be displayed in glass vitrines.

If a client has no special talismans, I encourage him to build on something he already enjoys looking at: watercolors, mugs, silver objects, miniature furniture, nineteenth-century paintings, photographs. Then it's not just me running around antique shops trying to find amusing things. Often a person just needs a germ of an idea to get started.

The most interesting spaces I know were usually assembled bit by bit, object by object, over the years rather than "finished" in one fell swoop. Like any task worth doing, building a collection takes time.

— *Tips for Displaying Collections* —

♦ As in real estate, location is everything: don't spend your hard-earned collection trivially. Find the right room, and within it the particular place that will best feature the qualities of the objects. Consider how the natural light and surrounding textures will bring out the colors and shapes.

♦ An intriguing collection can add grace and character to an entry or hallway. Secondary spaces are too often overlooked: a hallway can become a gallery.

♦ The creativity comes in finding an order that makes sense of the objects and lets them work together. Then they will catch and hold your attention as they eloquently tell a small story about the person who lives in this room.

PHOTOGRAPHS

I'm very partial to photographs, which can bring a very special visual and even intellectual heft to a room. You can't beat classic photos by Ansel Adams, Edward Steichen, Irving Penn, and Richard Avedon. Black-and-white photos work beautifully with the quiet palette I'm partial to—cream, beige, taupe or tan, gray, and charcoal. (I may do rooms with dark floors and white walls, but I never do black-and-white rooms—they're too stark for me.) Because of their graphic quality, black-and-white photographs are near cousins to line drawings. But if an interior calls out for something especially quiet, sepia-toned prints are perfect because they are both gentle and glamorous. I hang photos in a group, because it gives a room a solid organizational footing. It's nice to have a collection of four or six photographs about the same subject, such as flowers, fashion, or gardens. Lately, with new digital technology, the size of photographs has exploded, and you can now work with very dramatic large-format prints. The look is very contemporary, and it can stand up to a room otherwise packed with color.

FAMILY PHOTOGRAPHS Family pictures can make a big visual contribution if they're carefully framed and placed. Grouped on a table and framed in the same type of material, such as gilded wood or glass, they add texture, detail, and even sparkle, not to mention the warmth of personalities and family history. You can use them most easily in personal spaces, such as a nightstand in the bedroom or in bookcases in the study. Shelves give the frames an architectural order. My theory is that if you're collecting pictures of your children at different ages, you should put them in the same kind of frame: silver easel-back frames are always elegant and wood imparts warmth. Don't be eclectic and mix brass, Lucite, and other materials within the same grouping of frames, because the ensemble becomes a collection of frames rather than pictures.

Turn a leftover space into a gallery. A client's family photographs acquire stature when collected into symmetrical blocks set between the windows of a long hall lined with storage cabinets for linens on one side.

FINDING THE RIGHT PLACE

A great painting needs its own space. When you're hanging
distinguished works of art, you want to give them every opportunity
to speak out for themselves—no suffocation, please. There are many
ways of making a painting come alive, but it shouldn't be one more
component in the clutter. If you have a special painting you want to
treat with the respect due a Matisse, keep the furniture back and
construct a stage for it, isolating it on the wall. The right spot could
be above the fireplace, or over a piece of furniture, or just by itself.

But it can also form the logical conclusion of a space, like the end of a hall. Symmetries and axes can help emphasize a painting within a room, giving it prominence. When I use furniture to center a room, I often consummate the composition with a piece of art. I use furniture to lock art into a room. You cannot hang art until you have furniture: art follows furniture, not furniture, art. You have to stand in a room and test it. Look for the centerlines, and let the geometries point to the work. Everybody has to find his own level of embellishment, whether it's only three pieces in a room, one large and two small, or a corner filled with posters from the 1920s.

A work needn't always be the star of a room. It can work as an ensemble player, within a grouping. If you have a charming piece, let it make friends with the furniture. Don't try to match the colors of the painting to the colors in the upholstery—that drains its vitality. Sometimes the work needs to relate to architectural elements, like windows and doors. I strongly believe in editing rooms. If something isn't working, take it away.

One of the secrets for keeping art—and even rooms—alive is to rotate the works. If you're bored with a piece, rehang it somewhere else. Shifting art around, decontextualizing and recontextualizing it, lets you see it in different ways. If you loved it once, you can love it again.

There is plenty of opportunity for art beyond the living room, from the front entry to the bedroom and bath. Some rooms present viewing issues. Corridors are narrow, so you can't stand back, but perspective is working for you if you place works at the end. Bathrooms are humid, so you don't want to hang art that is easily damaged, especially works on paper. The kitchen doesn't usually offer much wall space because of the cupboards. Bedrooms

ROOMS

On a mantelpiece, objects instantly become art. Here, an architectural finial holds its own alongside a vintage print and a silver candlestick.

encourage more intimate art pieces—the works should be quieter, calming, and unaggressive, such as landscapes and drawings. The entry hall presents the first impression, and if there's enough space, it can be the gallery of the house.

How High Should You Hang It?

You can often tell the height of the owner of the house by the height of the paintings. The considerate owner hangs artwork at average eye level, which is about five feet six inches, especially if they are small works that invite close-up looking. Larger paintings allow more latitude, but you generally want your eyes level with the painting's center of gravity. Of course, take into consideration the other elements in a room, like chair rails, doors, and moldings, that alter the proportion of a wall.

There are several different systems of hanging besides the old nail in the wood stud. Some people are now placing paintings and photographs, especially small to medium-size pieces, on waist-high ledges built into walls. Leaning the works on the wall along the rail allows for easy changing and lends the room informality. The old system of hanging pictures from a hook attached to a molding at the top of a wall has long since been discredited: it's too difficult to change, and the wires create lines you don't want to see.

Most decorating is done for the adult world, but it's great fun to hang art for children at their own height. There's no better way to tell them that the art belongs to them too. They're really never too young. I began buying good starter art for my children early, and they've kept it. I gave pieces to them on their birthdays and also hung their own work to encourage their efforts—kids often have good work in their little portfolios. Children are born collectors, so I like to make shelves and places for their rocks, shells, and ceramics, so that the house anticipates and orders their treasures.

OPPOSITE
The foyer in this summer house is the setting for a brilliant marriage of art and textile—a painting of a Sagaponack field and a nineteenth-century American hooked rug.

ABOVE
A handsome mahogany screen with aerial views of Paris almost merges with a headboard and dramatizes this bed.

LEFT
Artwork was hung to create a consistent line in this hallway.

FRAMING

Of course, how and where you hang a piece depends on the size and type of frame. Here the variety of possibilities is mind-boggling, and sometimes counterintuitive. Small art in big frames can be magical, floating against a white background. But sometimes you want to snug the frame up to the art and eliminate any border altogether. I love big, heavily carved wooden frames, but they require a serious work of art to justify the elaborateness. I usually talk over the possibilities with an expert framer, who can weigh the needs of the room against the needs of the painting. If it's a work on paper, make sure the framer suggests a good way to cover the work to protect it against direct light, and even bounced light. You have to be very careful since color on paper is fugitive.

To find a good framer, look around and visit local framing shops. If you like what you see, bring in your piece and see what each framer suggests. Pick the one whose ideas are even better than yours.

I liked the contrast of the bold, rectangular lines of a French Directoire-style mirror above the curvaceous Italian console table. The eighteenth-century silver chalices have very strong forms and hold their own against both pieces of furniture.

LIGHTING

Paintings are created in natural light, and in a house they prosper in the same natural light. That said, you should never hang any work, not even an oil painting, on a wall struck by direct sunlight. I've seen even rugs fade to white in plate-glass houses where the light is uncontrolled. But with a reasonable amount of natural light, you don't have to install recessed cans everywhere on the ceiling to illuminate your art. If you hang something near a lamp, or above a sideboard with a pair of lamps on either end, the art will probably be adequately lit without getting too fussy about it. Besides, recessed lights built into a ceiling create a Swiss-cheese effect, especially when the casing around the bulbs is black. The better alternative is a silver or white casing. Track lighting is more appropriate for gallery-like interiors, and miniaturization has made recessed tracks possible: those little halogen spots are hardly discernible tucked up out of sight. Picture lights suit nineteenth-century art, which can be very dark; without some light on the surface, many of these pieces can't be seen on a gray day.

There's a type of physics to lighting, and if you opt for spotlights, you have to be careful about the spacing and type of lamps. Track lights are adjustable, of course, but recessed lights have to be placed at least thirty inches away from the wall to wash the paintings evenly and create enough bounce off the wall. They should be spaced not more than twenty-four inches apart to prevent shadows and scallops from appearing on the wall and

209

THE ART OF LIVING
WITH ART

paintings. Dimmers are very useful for adapting artificial light to the natural light available and for controlling the mood of a room. You needn't look at a painting with the light on full blast all the time but can vary the intensity with the dial. Just as you don't want aggressive lighting on people, you don't want it on paintings. I hate the harsh lighting that so many people live with.

As for those little sketches that I bought at Doyle's, I kept them in their envelope and carried them around, like a treasure, showing them to friends. I found out that the artist, Abraham Walkowitz, was an early modern American painter who worked primarily in the 1920s and 1930s. As I said, the sketches are small, just three-by-five-inch studies, and I finally opted to do a proportionate framing. I didn't want them to swim against too much matting. I decided to exaggerate their presence in a flat modern frame that would catch a lot of light and animate them a little. I didn't want the frame to compete. I grouped them several to a frame and decided that the drawings merited the cost of gold leaf. I stored them behind the couch in bubble wrap and sneaked peeks at them until, finally, the right wall for them came into my life. I hung them in my bedroom in Remsenburg, low on two separate walls near my bed so that I can enjoy them up close while I read. Because of their scale and the softness of the pencil, proximity is important. They keep each other, and me, company.

A mural is a long-neglected art form, and if you're brave enough to commission one, it will enhance your room.

9. LESS AND MORE

If you are going to single out an accessory, select one with a history.

BILLY BALDWIN, a legendary American decorator who brought a new clarity to traditional style, used to tell a story. Every time he stepped into the salon of the country club he had designed, he couldn't figure out what was wrong with the room. Then one day he walked over to the couch and removed the pillows. Suddenly the whole place looked so much better. It just goes to show that even the smallest object, like the wrong pillow, has a power far beyond its size and can break up the harmony you've worked so hard to achieve.

I grew up in a small town in the Midwest where anything unnecessary was considered excessive, and I'm from the school of those who take away. When you pare down, you achieve a kind of purity. A table laden with a collection of pottery creates a different effect than one set with a single object. Of course, that solitary object has to be beautiful. If you're going to single out an accessory, select one with a history. It should be meaningful to you. Nothing can hide when a room is simple: If the pieces stand out, they have to stand on their own.

PREVIOUS PAGES
More: a collection of fifteen French pressed botanicals.

ABOVE
If you want to celebrate a collection of objects, open the doors.

OPPOSITE
What could be simpler: a bowl, a vase, and an early American weathervane.

EDITING

Pared-down usually means less furniture, less decoration, and simple solutions. In color, it might mean either a neutral, monochromatic environment or a room done in no more than two hues. With bouquets, it means one type of flower in the same color rather than all kinds of flowers in every shade. Likewise, in decorating, paring down requires that you resist the urge to clutter surfaces and indulge in all sorts of patterns, whether it's on the furniture, walls, or floors. Forget covering the sofa and chairs in a bevy of chintz. Some people want to comfort themselves with a lot of objects and visual fuss, but I'm not productive when I'm surrounded with toile wallpaper. I close the door on audiovisual equipment by stashing it in an armoire instead of putting it out on a shelf. Who wants to see all those dials?

There's a fine line between complexity and simplicity, and you can push it in either direction and get beautiful results. If the visual stimulation is controlled and elegant, I can live with surplus. Swags, jabots, and trimmed taffeta curtains can be just as lovely as clean-lined solar screens and diaphanous muslin at the windows—it all depends on what mood you want. Be aware of your own tastes and limits, and try to reflect your own personality in ways that make you feel

comfortable. A spare, pared-down room that seems serene to some people might strike others as totally neurotic. Given the choice of a Christian Lacroix dress or a Calvin Klein sheath on a rack, which would you reach for?

Less rather than more is a matter of taste rather than period. British designer John Pawson, perhaps today's most well-known Minimalist, and the austere Shakers both share an aversion to ornament. They have a lot in common besides style. A pared-down room doesn't have to be purely contemporary. You can find many examples of a clean, simple look down through the centuries—open a history book and glance at some pictures of an Irish Georgian manor or an American Federal house. I inhabit both camps and like to incorporate elements of each into my designs. Just because you admire that spare, pared-down look doesn't mean you have to choose between traditional and contemporary. It's not that one's right and the other's wrong.

OPPOSITE
Two equally stylish foyers, one modest and one flamboyant.

ABOVE
You can decide to either hide all the audiovisual equipment or build a temple to the silver screen.

LESS	MORE
SIMPLE, SPARE: *white rooms*	COMPLEX, FULL: *dark walls*
CONTROLLED: *Shaker furniture*	SPONTANEOUS: *Italian furniture*
QUIET: *linen slipcovers, muslin curtains*	ANIMATED: *chintz upholstery, silk draperies*
UNADORNED: *hand-loomed rug*	EMBELLISHED: *Persian carpet*
RESTRAINED SCALE: *iron lantern*	DRAMATIC SCALE: *Venetian glass chandelier*
EASY: *pine planks*	GRAND: *mosaic floors*

ADDITION AND SUBTRACTION For people who find comfort in abundant, generous rooms, editing is a matter of addition rather than subtraction. This is a different kind of art, and not at all easy. It requires discipline. You have to be careful not to go over the top. (Remember those overstuffed Victorian rooms with red-flocked wallpaper and potted palms?) But at its best, the *abbondanza* effect is as delicious as the complex flavor of a wine or stew. The trick is knowing which spices to put in, how they will complement each other, and when one more would be too much. I often add color or pattern to lift a room and give it more life. It could be just a little check or a stripe on a pillow or two, in compatible colors. When I add something, I usually do it within a limited range that's already been established. For example, I might skirt an existing ottoman or pick a rosebud pattern for the canopy on a four-poster bed. I always avoid high contrast because I believe that incremental differences give you richness without jarring contradictions. You never want to break the tone of the room.

OPPOSITE AND BELOW
Less and more: Marblehead
pottery versus a replica of a
Chinese porcelain shop.

Three approaches to
a mantel: one object
(opposite), more objects
(above), and a collection
of objects (left).

If you bring in a secretary bookcase and open it to display a collection of inkwells, you add another layer to the room.

OPPOSITE

In this library there is a quiet simplicity of line.

CORRECTIONS AND ADJUSTMENTS

Some people can visualize how a table or a fabric will look in a certain setting, and others can't tell until they see it in place at home. I spend months planning each room down to the last detail until I've got it all worked out in my mind. But each time we install a room, there are inevitably a few surprises— sometimes good and sometimes bad. When all the furniture finally

arrives, there's often a need for adjustments, such as moving a lamp or taking away a table. Fabric can be especially tricky because you've selected it from a sample; in reality, a mass of fabric is very different from a swatch. The lighting conditions of your house won't replicate those in the store or showroom, so you'll be seeing the finished upholstered pieces in literally a different light.

If something doesn't quite work, don't be afraid to change it. Creativity is never cut and dried, and you have to be flexible enough to adjust your plan. You shouldn't be married to every piece of furniture. Rooms, like our lives, should evolve. Every time you move or redecorate, there will be some old things that you'll keep and other pieces that never quite worked. Finally, you may be able to throw them away. Weeding out can be difficult, but it usually bears fruit.

OPPOSITE BOTTOM
City savvy.
OPPOSITE TOP
Penthouse chic.
ABOVE
Country charm.

IF THERE'S SOMETHING WRONG WITH YOUR ROOM
AND YOU DON'T KNOW WHAT IT IS, TRY:

- Removing a pillow or two.

- Changing the lightbulbs, which may be too bright or too dim.

- Putting all the lights on a dimmer so that you can vary the atmosphere.

- Changing the curtains.

- Getting rid of any color that screams for attention and takes your eye away from everything else.

- Taking away one object, and then another if that doesn't do the trick.

- Reallocating family photos to private areas.

- Removing that pile of coffee-table books.

- Getting rid of those fussy finials on the lamps.

- Changing the lampshades.

- Tossing the scented candles in favor of plain white votives.

- Throwing an ottoman in, where you might want to put your feet up.

- Slipcovering an unfortunate upholstery job.

ROOMS

Less: one landscape above the bed.

IO. Finishing Touches

*Never underestimate the impact
of those final comforting touches.*

PREVIOUS PAGES
Keep your eyes open for little jewels, such as these crystal finials, which could dress up a plain-Jane staircase.

BELOW
A Victorian beadwork stool is a delicate accent in a bedroom.

GRACE NOTES can make all the difference in a piece of classical music, and a room is no different. Never underestimate the impact of those final comforting touches. An intricately embroidered pillow; a soft, warm shawl; a handsome pair of lamps; or a distinctive stool can help pull a room together and add another layer of personality. Accent pieces may seem superficial, but they have a surprising power to complete the picture. You can't build a room without first thinking about structure, but you need more than structure to make it sing.

Window
Treatments

How you dress a window can range from
minimal and inexpensive to elaborate and
dear, but in either case the overall treatment
will occupy a large part of your field of vision.
The window wall of a room is the back of the
facade, the transition between outside and
inside. Windows normally occupy one-
quarter to one-third of their walls, so they
play a major part in the design. A room is
going to look pretty bare unless you put
something on them, and at night the
windows will go black, throwing off the
balance of color and light you've tried so
hard to achieve. Besides, unless you have
great views, windows can be an eyesore
without something beautiful to soften them.

Because of their potential impact, windows present a great
design opportunity, and there is a vast range and variety of easily
available treatments. Drapery at either side of the opening is,
of course, the most common way to treat a window, but Roman
shades often take their place; the fabric rides up on a string so
that it folds onto itself in layers as it rises. The balloon shade,
the dressiest drapery alternative, forms a glorious waterfall.

TOP
Curtains can hide an
unfortunate view or quietly
frame a verdant landscape.
ABOVE
They can be trimmed with
satin or left unadorned to
fall gracefully to the floor.

You can lift a room out of the ordinary with an unusual light fixture like this French wrought-iron chandelier.

A contemporary version of the shade that rides up a set of strings is the duette—a very affordable, double-sided folding blind made of paper or fabric, with an air cavity that blankets the window for thermal protection. Duettes are very flexible: you just walk into a store with the window dimensions and have the shades fabricated to size. They take up very little space when folded and come in a gazillion different colors and materials, including gauzy ones, which I like.

Of course, you have the option of combining treatments and arranging them in layers; the effect is more formal and usually costs more. With a multiple treatment, you start with a structure, like a drapery panel built up to the window frame in double or even triple fullness, to encompass the width of the window when drawn. A valance overhead ties the two panels together. I like a plain valance with a kick pleat in each corner. A popular alternative to the valance these days is a plain metal rod mounted at the top of the window. The idea is directness and simplicity, and you can put together the hardware inexpensively by combing the racks at outlets like Home Depot or Lowe's.

Typically, for a layered look that gives you several alternatives, use both undercurtains and overcurtains, all set within a structure that includes side panels as well as a valance. For a dressy living room, you might hang draperies over Roman shades, or you might simplify the undercurtains, using any of the huge number of sheers available, everything from cottons to wools to linens to polyesters. Sheers, or "nets," as the Brits call them, give you diffused light and privacy. A filmy fabric can cut the glare and make direct sunlight incandesce, turning something harsh into something glowing— all the while veiling the outside and softening unwanted views. In period rooms, or rooms with more elaborate molding, it's tempting to go for sumptuous, baroque curtains, trimmed with fringe. But then everything else in the room has to live up to that gesture; otherwise, the emphasis on the windows is disproportionate. In the 1980s window treatments often went over the top, but since then they've gone on a diet. I rarely use a heavy pattern at the window, though I would choose a color and fabric that play into the color scheme of the walls and upholstery. Often I let the furniture determine the draperies; antiques, for example, suggest using curtains with a handmade quality. In historical houses, you can decorate one or two rooms with swags and jabots and remain true to the character of the period.

A major factor determining your choice is the quantity of light. With a bright exposure, you probably need to diffuse the light with a solar screen or parchment shade or maybe just an old-fashioned pull-down shade (though with grips on each side, to avoid that annoying little string dangling in the middle). The solar-screen shade comes in many degrees of perforation, ranges from diaphanous to opaque, and gives a clean, more modern look. In a formal bedroom you might combine an off-white parchment shade with a blackout shade for daylight sleeping—these no-light shades are much more sophisticated and varied than they used to be.

Blinds and curtains diffuse not only light but darkness. You might decide not to dress the windows in a modernist room because the surrounds are crisp, like a starched collar. But without shades of some kind, the windows become black holes draining the energy from a room at night. If you don't want a window treatment to spoil the architectural lines, illuminate the yard outside to eliminate the night inside.

SHUTTERS I think of shutters as a small architectural element, like moldings. The range of choices is surprisingly large, from the size of the blades to the number of hinged panels. Usually the dimension of the shutters corresponds to the size of the window frame, but shutters can be subdivided—broken into lowers and uppers, for example. You might want privacy below but full light above, and dividing the height lets you operate both registers independently. You can play with scale by choosing bifold or trifold panels: the narrower the width, the taller the shutters and windows appear, giving the room an illusion of height. Single panels with wide blades evoke the breezy ways of the tropics, while smaller shutters convey a more sophisticated, urbane feeling. In nineteenth-century buildings, shutters were often built into town houses to provide privacy on the lower floors and were frequently used in association with other window treatments. Shutters are particularly well suited to a library—paint or stain them to match the wood paneling if you have it. For a lot of brightness inside, keep shutters light. I think pure wooden shutters should be left to the Aesthetic Movement, but their close cousin, wooden Venetian blinds, natural or painted and suspended on cotton straps, can be unexpected and fresh in the right application—as in a midcentury modernist house.

You can't pull stationary curtains across French doors or windows without making the door or window inoperative. So I came up with this solution—curtains that move right along with the door. I stretch linen from two swinging rods to make shutter-like shades.

ACCENTS

Accents are the salt and pepper that enhance the taste of a room.

An accent piece could be anything that's exceptional or different in a room, whether small or large, old or new, traditional or modern— a crocheted pillow, a tasseled fringe, crystal beads on a lampshade, a little hooked rug by the fire, match strikers, a Noguchi lamp. As classical as my rooms are, I live for eccentricity, for creating that dash in space. Unless there is something off, a room has no energy. A businessman dressed in a gray suit, white shirt, and dark tie has no buzz, but pour him into a blue shirt with a spiffy Hermès tie and he comes alive. There's no sure formula for turning the dial of a room off-center, but an unexpected color—such as robin's egg

blue, orangey-yellow, celadon green—on a beautiful piece of porcelain is a good start. If not color, it could be an accent texture: a collection of silver boxes could work as an accent, shimmering in the light. Pillows, of course, are a tried and true way of accenting a room, but that odd-fabric-out could also be needlepoint on a stool, or a shawl tossed over the shoulder of a sofa.

I can throw a room to the left by bringing in an unusual chair. It might have an S-shaped profile or be upholstered in a saturated green. The idea is that this character piece is not related to any other style in the room. In a modern space, you would slip in a baroque piece, or in a traditional room, a modern piece. It's the exception rather than the rule that gives the space energy. Of course, proportion matters: if the accent is too overwhelming, it becomes the subject, and the foreground migrates to the background. Accents are the salt and pepper that enhance the taste of a room.

BELOW FROM FAR LEFT
Pillows are a boon to the back and a pleasure to the eye; get out the needle and thread and add a tassel trim to your favorite reading chair; instead of the conventional crystal chandelier, try an iron lantern; a vivid color sets off the upholstered headboard and tailored linens.

LAMPS Lamps ought to be simple—good quality and beautiful design, yes, but I don't like them to be so ostentatious that they take your eye away from the complete picture. If you need some color balance in a room, a Chinese red or cobalt blue lamp will provide a vivid note, whether in an old or new environment. The forms can be either traditional or as abstract as a Brancusi, but I avoid those cute little porcelain figures you often see on lamps: at a distance, they weaken the form and rob the basic color of its impact. I never get cute with my lamps; I'd never stick a lampshade on an antique toy drum. My preference in lamps is for clean forms, pure colors, and simple materials.

Of course, there are lots of different ways to light a room. You're off to a good start if you light a space from the four corners out. If you don't illuminate the corners, you will always have a shadow there. If there's not enough room for table lamps, use floor lamps. To provide a comfortable spot for reading, put floor lamps next to the most likely chairs, and others on tables in close proximity.

Lampshades are a world unto themselves: they run the gamut in style and material from painted metal, parchment, beads, and opaque paper to pleated or stretched silk. They have another dimension, however, that's easily forgotten because it's so subtle. Shades color the light emitted from a bulb and give a room its connotation. Parchment warms up a room, while a shade lined

OPPOSITE
Take a risk. Show off your personality with a leopard-skin chair.
ABOVE
Original 1940s sconces by French designer Jean Royère.

with blush-pink silk gives a glow. Pure white shades cool a room and subtract a little color from the palette, particularly if you use a clear bulb. A frosted bulb will diffuse the light and cut the harshness. Off-white shades make everything look gentler. Lampshades have a special ability to define the scale of a room. Floating in space, they establish its virtual height.

Make sure the light in a room is balanced. You generally want lamps to be at one or two levels so that they don't jump up and down and make a room visually nervous. If the lighting is harsh in any way, use dimmers to create a gentler level of light. Paintings, especially big contemporary works, require bright and somewhat clinical light, which you'll want to counterbalance with warm lamplight.

Overhead light is harsh (and works well only in dining rooms, kitchens, and baths); if you displace it to the side, as in a sconce, it's less intrusive. Sconces offer a room more than just light. They are accent pieces that, when paired or multiplied, give a room geometry and formal rhythm. They point up and even help create a sense of architecture in a room. On either side of a fireplace or a mirror, they add a little more formality. It's always nice to have a sconce next to a small mirror because the light is doubled by the reflection. In early American houses, candles placed in front of a concave silver dish projected more light. Sconces placed roughly at eye level give you a second height in a room and bring down the scale.

TABLESCAPES I select objects for the tops
of tables as carefully as I select furniture for
a room. You don't need to go out and buy
masses of things; just five objects in a range
of scales will do. If you have a table, you need
to have things on it in order to give it a
purpose, so that it plays a role in the space.
Table sculpture or objets d'art can animate
a room. Though good pieces are hard to find,
there's always something engaging at flea
markets—like Italian glassware or 1940s
pottery, which is plentiful because it was mass-
produced. The table is a place where you can
express a lot of personality in a concentrated
way. It's surprising how much impact that
small elevated plateau can have on a room.

If you rarely use your dining room, it can
be the most deadly room in the house. Think
about how your table looks when guests aren't
eating there. Build up something relevant in the
center, like a big bowl that anchors the table,
and take care that the chairs have a life of their
own, with slender backs perhaps, or cloudlike
curves. Outfit the sideboard too—it's like a
serving tray of objects—building it up as the
pedestal of a composition that might include a mirror above.

Of course, the table setting itself—the china, crystal, silver,
candelabra—is a great opportunity to strut your stuff. It's a
temporary work, a little like an art installation, but it leaves a
permanent impression.

FLOWERS Everyone usually trusts flowers to bring a room to life, but it's easier said than done. Somehow flowers get used up: your eye tires and no longer registers blooms that have been overexposed. So bouquets that are considered exotic now may not be refreshing next year. You have to mix things up, since the wrong flowers can wreak havoc in a room.

Physically, flowers should be the right scale for the room and in the right-size vase: they don't work if they're too short, too tall, or skimpy. Plastic flowers, of course, never work, and silk flowers rarely do. But at their best, flowers bring color, shape, and volume to a space. Usually, a pair of vases brimming with poppies on the mantel, or a cornucopian arrangement of twisting tulips on a table, or one small luxurious bouquet of anemones on a coffee table, is enough to animate the space. But you can't have flowers everywhere. They have to be subtle enough to coexist as a companion to everything else in a room, or strong enough to be an accent. I find potted plants a little ordinary, unless they're orchids, and even then you have to be careful not to be too showy.

You won't go wrong if you always come back to the idea of balance. The same principle that governs the room as a whole also applies to these finishing touches. Accents like a Swedish glass bowl or a pair of candlesticks should not overwhelm a room, but simply enhance it, reinforcing its symmetry and style.

LEFT

A tablescape can be a moving picture show. Something like this pre-Colombian pot will stay for a while, then suddenly I'll move everything around and come up with a whole new composition.

OPPOSITE

Peonies, little boxes, and vintage children's books—these are a few of my favorite things.

AFTERWORD: A Room of One's Own

When people tell me that my rooms are serene, I'm especially pleased, because I think we need to establish pockets of calm in a world that's too much with us. That same serenity draws me to Renaissance paintings, and I'm sure it's their underlying order, the intersecting circles, triangles, and squares, that contributes to that feeling even after centuries. It's no accident: the paintings are composed. But it would be wrong to assume that the calm is static.

In Renaissance art the underlying geometries lead your eye all over the canvas, and that's exactly what I want in my rooms. The final test is that the eye never stops dead, with nowhere else to go, but is always led somewhere else, by the geometries, textures, and light. The sum total is intriguing. I keep the eye moving as it completes a virtual circle within the room. The appeal of such symmetry is simple—it leaves us with a sense of

Elegant casement windows wrap this sunporch. The curtains, made out of inexpensive bridal lace and tulle, drape every wall and window and billow languidly in the breeze.

tranquillity. But the circumstances are complex—you walk into a room that reads as a rich tableau.

The pairs and symmetries register so clearly because I've learned how to eliminate clutter. My classical bent is informed by modernism, and I always simplify, reducing rooms to the essentials. I surround each piece with enough space to let it breathe. Furniture moves off the walls and toward the room's center, where it can be seen from all sides—like sculpture. Modern pieces rub shoulders with antiques.

You can't pin down my rooms as traditional or contemporary. I modernize the classical and classicize the modern. The two great design movements that came roaring through the twentieth century are not opposed or contradictory, as we all have been led to believe. They can fuse right in front of your fireplace, as a lean traditionalism or a relaxed modernism. You can adopt the advantages of both.

It's all right to be in the middle. You don't have to pare all your possessions down to the bare minimum or cover every cushion in striped silk. You make your choices and find your own style. People tend to think that design is for others—for the professionals or the more affluent. But some of the best things in a room are free. Now that you have a map through the process, all you need is imagination. You're ready to build a room of your own.

A towering tole pagoda was the unexpected touch that lifted the room to new heights of fancy.